Unraveling
Faculty
Burnout

Unraveling Faculty Burnout

Pathways to Reckoning and Renewal

REBECCA POPE-RUARK, PhD

JOHNS HOPKINS UNIVERSITY PRESS

BALTIMORE

Johns Hopkins University Press
2715 North Charles Street
Baltimore, Maryland 21218-4363
www.press.jhu.edu

Library of Congress Cataloging-in-Publication Data

Names: Pope-Ruark, Rebecca, author.
Title: Unraveling faculty burnout : pathways to reckoning and renewal /
  Rebecca Pope-Ruark, PhD.
Description: Baltimore : Johns Hopkins University Press, 2022. |
  Includes bibliographical references and index.
Identifiers: LCCN 2021062995 | ISBN 9781421445120 (paperback) |
  ISBN 9781421445137 (ebook)
Subjects: LCSH: College teachers—Job stress—United States. | College
  teachers—Job satisfaction—United States. | College teacher turnover—
  United States—Prevention. | Burn out (Psychology)—Prevention.
Classification: LCC LB2333.3 .P67 2022 | DDC 378.1/20973—dc23/eng/20220110
LC record available at https://lccn.loc.gov/2021062995

A catalog record for this book is available from the British Library.

*Special discounts are available for bulk purchases of this book. For more information, please
contact Special Sales at specialsales@jh.edu.*

For all those who shared their stories with me

and for those who could not

Contents

Unraveling
Faculty
Burnout

Burnout

An Unraveling or a Reckoning?

No one wants to burn out, but we
are all living like we are on fire.

—Brené Brown

I sat across from my new therapist, clutching a sofa pillow to my chest and silently fuming that I had to be there. At a recent yearly physical I had admitted to being depressed, but only because I couldn't seem to concentrate anymore. It was the end of a difficult academic year, and I had just had a breast cancer scare (thankfully, just a scare), so of course I was tired and worn out. I knew that if I could just regroup and concentrate, I would come out of this funk and get back to business. I had a pilot program to run, a new major to grow, a special issue of a major disciplinary journal to put together, and a contract for an edited collection with a very well respected university press to develop. My physician advised me to see a psychiatrist to discuss different pharmaceutical options and to meet with a local therapist she recommended.

I'd been to therapy before. During bouts of anxiety through my master's and doctoral program years, I had found therapy to be somewhat helpful. But I've led a fortunate life; what did I have the right to complain about? Good childhood with loving parents. Great education. Loving and supportive husband. My dream job and tenure at a private liberal arts–focused university. Strong publication record and a book with a major academic press.* Whining to someone about feelings would not make anything better—I just needed to suck it up and figure out how to concentrate again.

I put off making the recommended appointments for two months, until my husband finally took the choice out of my hands. He worked from home the day of my first therapy appointment and ~~threatened~~ offered to drive me there. So I went. If I could persuade the therapist that all I needed was some Ritalin or Adderall to concentrate, I would be fine.

Laura seemed nice enough. She asked me some get-to-know-you questions and about my current state of mind. I explained that I'm overly stressed at work with a lot to do and that I was struggling to concentrate, which was making everything worse. I had important shit to do, which I explained in lengthy detail, focusing on the must-dos and should-dos among my responsibilities. About midway through the session, Laura asked me how long I had been unhappy at my job. Without really thinking, I blurted out, "Seven years." That stopped me short. Had I really been miserable for so long? Laura just let that sit for a while, so it had time to penetrate my thick professional shell.

There had certainly been some trying times during those seven years. For example, there had been a departmental schism when my colleagues and I tried (unsuccessfully) to spin out of our department. More recently, the spring 2017 pilot of the new design-thinking program I had put my heart and soul into had been emotionally and professionally traumatic. I dreaded going to campus for any reason. Now, students were just emotionally exhausting, and I didn't want to deal with their perennial problems. I avoided colleagues and meetings as much as

---

* People were often impressed that I published my book with the University of Chicago Press, but it took me a long time to break the habit of responding with, "It's just a faculty development book, not actual scholarship." Not being able to enjoy your accomplishments is a hallmark of burnout.

possible, especially conversations that would likely include conflicts or battles I was tired of fighting. I hadn't written anything for months, which was devastating to me as a writing teacher and professional writer. But I told myself and Laura that if I could just concentrate long enough to write, to get the scholarship about the pilot program out there, it would make the experience worthwhile, and I would prove to myself that it hadn't beat me.

After I asked again for probably the hundredth time for ADD medicine to help me concentrate and get back to work, knowing full well that she could not actually prescribe medication, Laura looked at me and said,

> You're smart enough to know that won't help. Your inability to concentrate is a symptom, not the problem. All of your symptoms—lack of concentration, sense of dread about teaching your classes and going to meetings, deep shame about not "producing" enough in the last year, anxiety attacks on your way to work and while unlocking your office door—you have *burnout*. Probably severe. The depression and anxiety are by-products. You can't run from that anymore. And if you keep running, you might not come back.

Basically, she said that my entire way of thinking about myself and doing my work might be causing irreparable damage to my mental health. Me, the person who had literally written a book on faculty vitality and productivity strategies. If the psychiatrist confirmed this diagnosis when we had our first appointment a month later, I would officially be a complete fraud. How could I promote the book or keep up with my blog or start a consulting side gig when I couldn't follow my own advice? My entire identity was wrapped up in my roles as teacher, scholar, writer. It was an identity that hinged on constantly *doing* work rather than living a life. What was I without all that?

For a long time, all I felt was what Laura labeled shame. Weakness. Fear—terror really—that someone would find out what I was going through and out me as a washout. My career and therefore my life were certainly ruined, because I wasn't strong enough to pull myself out of this mental mess and remain the professional I showed the world. Burnout felt like a career death sentence.*

Now I know that I am not alone.

How Is Faculty Vitality a Journey Rather Than a Goal?

In my first book, *Agile Faculty: Practical Strategies for Managing Research, Service, and Teaching* (2017), I argued for faculty vitality through meaningful productivity. According to the research, vital faculty embody "challenge seeking, creativity, curiosity, energy, grit, growth mindset, motivation, optimism, and risk taking [as well as] productivity" (DeFillipo and Giles 2015, 2). These faculty are engaged and passionate throughout their careers, are driven by their short- and long-term goals, and pursue professional growth opportunities over time (Baldwin 1990, 172, 174). And vital faculty feel "a sincere commitment to both individual and institutional goals, [derive] satisfaction from professional endeavors, [manifest] behaviors that reflect enthusiasm for intellectual activity, and [look] forward to what the future may bring" (Gooler 1991, 8).

---

* Catastrophizing was one of my most frequently used anxiety outlets. Everything was always life or career death. Everything was going to end terribly. I'd lose my job, which was the only thing I was ever good at; I would fail in the "real world," as I had in my twenties; everyone thought I was shrill, unlikable, and condescending (another awesome anxiety thinking pattern). Being inside my head was not fun.

What I didn't talk about in *Agile Faculty* is the fact that constantly trying to live up to all these ideals is exhausting, unrealistic, and potentially dangerous. A long career comprises many seasons, peaks, and valleys. Life goes on around us and sometimes brings struggle—with health, family and caregiving, economic or social challenges. The academic job market is brutal, often leaving highly qualified, wonderful colleagues on the outside struggling to stitch together a living off the tenure track. Many midcareer faculty find themselves wondering what comes next after earning tenure and/or promotion. Male-dominated fields remain unwelcoming to women, and faculty of color put in significantly more unrecognized emotional labor with students and mentees, which is draining and takes time away from other work, than white colleagues. And if you teach traditional undergraduates, you get older while they stay exactly the same age. And even situations and relationships that had felt safe in the past can sour.

Over the intense months of self-work following my first therapy appointment, I came to understand that my entire self-worth was wrapped up in my scholarly productivity and external validation in the forms of awards, teaching evaluations, publications, and service leadership. How did I get to this point? It happened slowly but then all at once. I have always been driven by outward markers of success that offered concrete goals to pursue relentlessly. I've also been so completely caught up in climbing the ladder that I fell prey to what Todd Henry (2013) calls "expectation escalation," a mind-set that permeates academia. My self-talk looked something like this:

You got that great tenure-track job in your field at your dream school? You got lucky; now, get tenure, publish in top journals, teach amazing classes, and become a leader in your disciplinary organization. Got tenure? Good for you; why haven't you published a book yet? You

need to publish more, teach even better classes and completely rede-
sign the program, run at least one major committee, and get national
recognition in order to get promoted to full. Oh, you wrote a book? It
was just a faculty development book, and you got lucky with that prestigious press. Where's the second book? Why aren't you directing a
research center by now? Have you peaked? Are you still relevant?

I measured my career according to ever higher and more unrealistic
productivity expectations, thinking I was lucky to have this calling and
a job anyone would fight for. No one stopped me from working myself
into the ground or told me they were worried that I might be pushing
myself too hard. Even if they had, I probably would not have listened. I
was sick a lot, but I said it was allergies and chronic migraine, not exhaustion. I was so high-functioning that I looked like I had it totally
together from the outside. But on the inside, "what started out as
important, meaningful, and challenging work [became] unpleasant, un-
fulfilling, and meaningless. Energy turn[ed] to exhaustion, involvement
turn[ed] to cynicism, and efficacy turn[ed] into ineffectiveness" (Maslach,
Schaufeli, and Leiter 2001, 416).

Burnout.

I let no one see that I was struggling, and I would never have asked
for help had I not had panic attacks in the presence of a senior colleague,
then my chair, and ultimately my dean. I was about as far from a "vital"
faculty member as I could get. And I didn't even want to *be* a faculty
member anymore. But what else could I possibly be? Could I be useful
anywhere else? Could I even imagine that?

Career vitality as an academic is a journey that requires us to be not
only agile but also human and vulnerable at times, states of being that I
refused to acknowledge in myself for too long and that higher ed culture actively stigmatizes. But the more we acknowledge that everything

is not always awesome in higher ed and the more we normalize paying attention to faculty wellness and well-being, the less shameful it will be to not always feel vital. And when we start to diminish the shame associated with individual physical and mental health challenges, the more ready we will be not only to take care of ourselves and our colleagues but also to change the culture that creates the burnout and shame in the first place.

What Is Burnout?

Discussing burnout among faculty is difficult, not only because we are trained to resist any visible sign of weakness but also because we don't have the language or tools to have those conversations. For years, I would commiserate with my colleagues about being "burned out" at the end of a semester or academic year. We would wear it as a badge of honor to feel included in the cult of busyness that has cursed so many of us to fetishize productivity and reputation, not questioning the systemic structures feeding this perspective.

Burnout in the clinical sense is a different beast than end-of-year exhaustion. While burnout does not yet appear in the American Psychological Association's *Diagnostic and Statistical Manual of Mental Disorders* (*DSM*) as a clinical diagnosis, it is included by the World Health Organization (WHO) in the *International Classification of Diseases* (ICD) versions 10 and 11. After defining burnout as a "state of vital exhaustion" in ICD-10, the WHO expanded its definition in ICD-11 to identify it as a *syndrome* that results from

> chronic *workplace stress* that has not been successfully managed. It is characterized by three dimensions: 1) feelings of energy depletion or exhaustion; 2) increased mental distance from one's job, or feelings of

negativism or cynicism related to one's job; and 3) reduced professional efficacy. Burnout *refers specifically to phenomena in the occupational context* and should not be applied to describe experiences in
other areas of life. (WHO 2019, emphasis added)

The WHO's definition aligns with the research of the organizational
psychologist Christina Maslach and her colleagues, the preeminent
scholars on burnout in the United States. Maslach, Wilmar Schaufeli,
and Michael P. Leiter (2001) argue that burnout is

a psychological syndrome in response to chronic interpersonal stressors on the job. The three key dimensions of this response are an overwhelming exhaustion, feelings of cynicism and detachment from the
job, and a sense of ineffectiveness and lack of accomplishment. (399)

Both the WHO and the Maslach team refer to burnout as a syndrome rather than a mental illness, with the latter arguing that instead
of being a "mental dysfunction," burnout can cause or exacerbate depression, anxiety, and other mental and physical health issues (2001,
406). For example, the *DSM* defines depression as marked by a consistent depressed mood and loss of joy or interest in life activities. To be
diagnosed with depression, a person must also experience at least four
of the following symptoms nearly every day: weight loss or gain; a
marked "slowing down of thought and a reduction of physical movement"; extreme fatigue; "feelings of worthlessness or excessive or inappropriate guilt"; an inability to concentrate or make decisions; suicidal
thoughts (WHO 2019). Many of these experiences are part of a burnout episode, including mine, but do not cause the burnout itself.

Burnout is specifically caused by chronic or unrelenting stress
associated with one's work, usually in one or more of the following

areas: workload, control, reward, community, fairness, values (Maslach, Schaufeli, and Leiter 2001, 414). As noted in the definitions above, three features are key to identifying burnout as separate from depression or anxiety:

> The *exhaustion* component represents the basic individual stress dimension of burnout. It refers to feelings of being overextended and depleted of one's emotional and physical resources. The *cynicism* (or *depersonalization*) component represents the interpersonal context dimension of burnout. It refers to negative, callous, or excessively detached response to various aspects of the job. The component of *reduced efficacy or accomplishment* represents the self-evaluation dimension of burnout. It refers to feelings of incompetence and a lack of achievement and productivity at work. (399, emphasis added)

Depression and anxiety often accompany burnout, and according to the Mayo Clinic (2021), if left unchecked, burnout can lead to fatigue and sleeplessness, drug and alcohol abuse, and physical health problems, including diabetes, high blood pressure, and heart disease. Women faculty members I spoke with added insomnia, acid reflux, unexplainable back pain, hypertension, and constant allergy-like symptoms, including food sensitivities. These symptoms can be both harbingers and consequences of burnout; even a person who is not diagnosed with burnout may still experience the symptoms as part and parcel of the syndrome. And left unchecked, these symptoms and consequences can be dangerous, as they were for me.

We'll explore these definitions and characteristics in more detail in the following chapters. Here, we will start with the position that burnout is a problem among faculty in higher education and my personal experience is not unique.

Why Is Burnout a Problem in Higher Education?

When I was first diagnosed with burnout, high-functioning depression, and severe anxiety, admitting to anyone what I was experiencing meant (to me) admitting that I was weak, phony, useless, and even used by others. But as I accepted my reality, I gained confidence to speak with trusted peers and share my burnout story. And the more people I talked to, the more stories* I heard:

Claire is a smart, driven, active doctoral student at a regional institution. As a graduate teacher of record for two undergraduate courses per semester, she reported to the director of the program for teaching assignments. After rebuffing two inappropriate advances, she found herself being bullied and denied reasonable requests for specific teaching times. She reported the behavior to the chair and ultimately the university, but that just made her supervisor angrier. Ultimately, she avoided campus as much as possible, teaching her classes and leaving immediately to work on her dissertation. By the time she passed her defense, she felt like a hollow shell of herself and was deeply concerned her mental state might follow her to her new assistant professorship.

The year Joanne earned tenure, she gave birth to her first child and purchased her first home with her partner. But she also experienced postpartum depression, exacerbated by the way mothering a newborn impacted her thinking and ability to focus. She knew from her reading that it might happen, but she didn't expect it to happen to her since her mind was her livelihood. Her partner was incredibly supportive and also a great parent to their daughter, but Joanne is stuck in a joyless

* Names and details have been changed throughout to protect the contributors' privacy. Stories may represent a composite of contributor experiences.

loop of feeling guilty for working when she "should be" mothering, and mothering when she "should be" working. Do other working moms in higher ed feel this bad all the time? she wondered.

Samantha had been at her institution for more than fifteen years, leading programs and serving as department chair, when she took a year-long research sabbatical in Europe. As a faculty member in a small program within a large department, she could do very little as she watched from afar as the larger factions voted against her program and advice repeatedly, until the program was ultimately eliminated. She very nearly did not return to the States because she found that her life and well-being were far more positive when she was far away from the repeated battles in her factionalized department. Ultimately, she only returned so that her twins could finish high school in the United States, but she and her partner were starting to plan a different life after the kids graduated.

After years of chasing publications and leadership roles, Rachel was eligible for promotion to full professor. But instead of starting to put her packet together, she found herself leaving campus immediately after class, even skipping meetings, to get home as soon as possible. She dreaded getting up in the morning and ran through a regular mental list to keep her from canceling class every day. She had regular panic attacks on and off campus. When she got home each day, she would play Solitaire on her phone for hours, avoiding grading and writing. She was used to being productive and engaged, so this new lethargy was totally humiliating.

Lucy taught ten courses, seven of which were new preps, during her two years on a teaching-track three-year appointment while also trying to finish dissertation revisions for her PhD defense. Her extended family experienced a devastating series of expected and unexpected deaths and other crises that year. She ended up traveling repeatedly across the country to handle these family matters, while still trying to keep up with work. Under all of this family and work pressure, she developed shingles and had no choice but to rest, hoping that her illness wouldn't make her contract renewal the next year even more precarious than it already was.

Keisha was the only Black professor in the nursing department. Although she worked at an urban, minority-serving institution, many of the faculty did not look like the student population. Keisha had taken the job because she loved working with minoritized first-generation college students like herself but also because the college was only a two-hour drive from most of her family. But as white supremacy and racial injustice dominated the news and her city, she was at her wit's end. Because she was the only person of color in the department, students regularly sought her out to discuss their own triggers and trauma. She remembered how important having Black professors and mentors had been to her, but taking on these students' trauma while experiencing her own was exhausting.

All these women's experiences led to burnout. Burnout can be experienced more deeply and regularly by women faculty for a variety of reasons. The sociologist Joya Misra builds on the challenges of the second shift, the expectation that women will do the majority of the care work for their families when they are not working: "It's important to recognize that as long as women are expected to do more of the care work, both inside and outside the workplace, women will be experiencing higher levels of burnout [than men]" (Flaherty 2020b).

One woman darkly joked with me about being the "housewife" in her male-dominated department, expected to organize any department gatherings and to manage anything related to food for events. The role was even more ironic to her because she was not tenured or on the tenure track but instead largely supporting her own position by bringing in more grants than anyone else in the unit.

In an article about faculty experiences with rejection, imposter syndrome, and burnout (Jaremka et al. 2020), the lead author, Lisa Jaremka, tells the heartbreaking story of being an assistant professor at an R1 institution who already felt overwhelmed when she went through her infertility journey:

> Some people implied that it was my fault for supposedly prioritizing my career over having children.... In theory, I could have taken a leave of absence as these and other significant personal stressors all unfolded. But as the primary breadwinner in my marriage, that was financially out of the question. And given my intense desire to succeed as a first-generation college student, this was also emotionally out of the question.... At times, it felt impossible to maintain productivity while also balancing these personal issues, and yet the tenure clock keeps ticking. (536)

None of these experiences are uncommon. A metastudy of burnout literature conducted by Jenny Watts and Noelle Robertson (2011) found differences in how men and women were likely to experience burnout. Several researchers determined that women were more likely to experience the emotional exhaustion of burnout, while men were more likely to withdraw or depersonalize (Ghorpade, Lackritz, and Singh 2007, 253; Lackritz 2004; Maslach, Jackson, and Leiter 1996). Perhaps because they "adapted to the threat of burnout" better or used healthier coping mechanisms, women faculty were more open about their experiences with others than their male colleagues (Pedersen and Minnotte 2017, 44–45). Daphne Pedersen and Krista Lynn Minnotte (2017) looked at burnout among STEM faculty in particular and found that women faculty were more impacted by unresolved work and interpersonal conflicts, resulting "in a hostile work environment for faculty women, who were labeled 'difficult' and hard to get along with" (57). Emily and Amelia Nagoski (2019) suggest that "women find profound satisfaction in understanding themselves and their identity in terms of relationships," so prolonged conflict can cause emotional exhaustion related to burnout: "Women's difficulty is rarely a lack of persistence" (147, 49).

How do we prevent, mitigate, or overcome burnout in a culture that creates the exact conditions required for burnout? We must first understand the cultural factors themselves and the behaviors they breed. But the COVID-19 pandemic certainly didn't help the situation.

COVID and Burnout

The COVID pandemic that swept the world in 2020 and 2021 had an immediate and deep impact on all facets of higher education, putting a spotlight on both physical and mental health. For faculty already hanging by a thread in the face of burnout, the crisis may have been too much to bear. Women and faculty of color have been especially hard hit, reporting exhaustion, frustration and cynicism, and a sense of futility, all three conditions of burnout, in potentially record numbers, according to a 2020 study conducted by Course Hero and reported in *Inside Higher Ed* (Flaherty 2020c).

As courses moved online, faculty began to work remotely where possible, and many research activities were curtailed, the unrelenting stress and uncertainty challenged mental health for both faculty and students. In a column in *Science* magazine, June Gruber and colleagues

(2020) argue, "Faculty burnout—exacerbated by pandemic-related stressors, absent childcare and school, and unrelenting or even accelerating work expectations from colleagues—poses real and serious risk for mental health challenges of unprecedented scope."

Perhaps one of the most obvious ways that women, faculty of color, and faculty who may earn less than working partners suffer is the crisis of absent child- and eldercare. Whereas daycare and school allowed faculty to work somewhat regularly during the day at least, the stress of not only having children or dependents home during the day with faculty parents but also having to homeschool at the same time led some directly into burnout.

Jessica Calarico, a sociologist at Indiana University, reported the toll the pandemic took on working mothers, finding that "88 percent say they're more stressed now than before the pandemic.... About one-third are getting less sleep ... and 47 percent report that they are getting more frustrated with their kids than before" (Flaherty 2020a). The realities of the academic job market regularly, if not usually, take faculty away from family and support networks that could have helped caregiving faculty balance work and childcare.

The *Chronicle* reporter Beth McMurtrie (2020) sums the situation up well:

> For some [faculty], the problem has been a crushing workload combined with childcare challenges. For others, it's feeling like their institution expects them to be counselors and ed-tech experts on top of their regular responsibilities, even if it means working seven days a week. Black and Latino professors are bearing additional burdens, supporting students of color and contributing to the national debate on racism. Meanwhile, adjuncts are barely hanging on, hoping that budget cuts don't end their careers.

As if burnout hadn't been as prevalent before the pandemic, we can now say that burnout is endemic in higher education.

Unhealthy Culture in Higher Ed

A major step toward eliminating burnout from the culture of higher ed is acknowledging that only systemic cultural changes will make a significant difference. Most of the reporting on burnout offers suggestions targeting individuals rather than the culture that led to the problem. Because burnout is endemic in higher education—and only increasing during the COVID-19 pandemic, creating possibly permanent changes in the careers of academics—individual interventions will not make a dent in the academic culture, especially for women and faculty of color.

Our culture values external rewards and ever-escalating and often competing expectations, all wrapped in the idea that we are fortunate to be in higher education in the first place. Being seen as someone who cannot keep up or is a troublemaker could be a death knell for the career of a serious academic. Reputation is *the* currency of the realm, a reflection of how busy we can make ourselves to look important, how often we can martyr ourselves at the altar of the discipline, or how much personal time and even our health we are ready to lay at the feet of the university, as well as how much the "popular kids" at the institution or your disciplinary conference like you. In a 2008 report, Kerry-Ann O'Meara, Aimee LaPointe Terosky, and Anna Neumann found that "even after receiving tenure, being excluded from many of the invisible colleges, 'intellectual parlors,' and significant disciplinary networks has left women and faculty of color bereft of critical learning opportunities" and hence potentially more vulnerable to burnout (51).

While one aim of this book is to normalize *talking* about burnout, it is not to normalize burnout as an acceptable cultural product (see also

Flaherty 2020b; Jaremka et al. 2020; and McMurtrie 2020). As Jonathan Malesic (2016) argues,

> Burned out faculty cannot be the teachers and mentors that students need them to be. As the profession becomes more economically precarious—with more and more adjuncts teaching for less and less money or recognition—the working conditions that foster burnout become more widespread. The quality of students' education and instructors' lives will spiral downward together if institutions don't face the problem. . . . The response to faculty burnout, therefore, should not be to shrug and say that academic work is a labor of love, and some just aren't cut out for it. Instead, the response should be to find ways to give these highly skilled workers the rest, respect, and reward they need to stay healthy and effective.

Vitality, Burnout, and Change

Hearing the stories from faculty peers across the different spectrums of higher education proved to me that I'm *not* weak or broken. As sad and, at times, enraging as the stories shared with me were, they helped to diminish the shame I was holding on to about my own burnout. I would never talk to these women who were bravely sharing their stories the way I talked to myself before I first confronted my burnout. Nor could there just be something "wrong" with these women given the volume of stories I heard.

If we understand our careers as an ongoing journey, times of high engagement, consistent meaningful productivity, and personal and professional satisfaction might represent the peaks, and burnout, poor mental health, deep cynicism about work, and emotional exhaustion might constitute the lowest of the lows on this path. But there is a great deal of middle ground to experience over the course of one's professional journey that doesn't necessarily lead to burnout. In my case, burnout forced me to take a long, hard look at myself as a person and professional and to make some changes to my life that I hadn't been quite brave enough to explore before.

Burnout led others to recommit to the goal that had been their original reason for choosing academia, to compassionately reconnect to themselves and their students, to overcome the fear of being publicly "found out," and to purposefully pursue balance between work and life. Some who saw burnout on the horizon were able to take steps to protect their physical health by demanding the support they needed and negotiating boundaries when asked to take on additional roles. Others, after much soul-searching, left academia by choice to pursue careers in industry, nonprofits, and entrepreneurial spaces after taking some time to improve their wellness.

Burnout does not necessarily extinguish vitality. What if vitality, self-image, and identity were not chained to productivity and reputation as the culture of higher ed, would that make us believe? What if we used our creativity, curiosity, resilience, motivation, and enthusiasm to (re)shape ourselves and the damaging culture of higher ed?

Why *Unraveling Faculty Burnout*?

A faculty member who succumbs to burnout is like the proverbial lobster added to a cool pot, who doesn't realize that the water is starting to boil. It creeps up on us slowly. Maybe we start dreading meetings, talking with students during office hours, or coming to work at all. Perhaps our physical or mental health begins to decline. Or maybe we become so jaded that we no longer see the point of our work. Some of us come out of it, some take positions at other institutions to shake themselves out, and others leave academia altogether, which has its own associated shame spiral given our indoctrination that higher education is a calling, not just a job. But it is. It's a job. Sometimes it's both, but it doesn't need to be.

While *Agile Faculty* offered strategies for facilitating career vitality through meaningful productivity, the purpose of this book is to get honest about the other end of that spectrum. If we acknowledge that feeling fulfilled and vital is not a singular destination, we (re)conceptualize vitality as an active journey that involves our hearts, hands, minds, and community of peers. Meaningful and realistic productivity is certainly a part of that journey, a part that may wax and wane at different decision points and stages of our careers, personal lives, health, and interests. While we are encouraged to share our peaks, a stigma is attached to talking about the valleys that keep many of us in higher education hiding in our own vulnerability.

Vulnerable is not a dirty word. It is a human word for a human feeling. It's how we deal with that vulnerability, or not, that helps to shape the professional vitality path we walk. *Unraveling Faculty Burnout* is not all doom and gloom, though it is honest and unflinching in the stories shared. I'm on the other side of this burnout episode, but I spent more than three years working on myself, interrogating my career focus, confronting the unhealthy identity I had developed for myself, and ultimately leaving a tenured position to work in faculty development two states away. I did this by focusing on what I've found to be four pillars of burnout resilience: knowing and following my *purpose*; practicing *compassion* for myself and others; deepening *connection* with peers near and far; and pursuing realistic life *balance*. Doing so took courage and resilience I wasn't sure I had, but I made it out the other side and am forever changed.

This book is also about acknowledging the cultural and individual factors that can lead to burnout and breaking the taboos by talking about it openly and honestly, by bringing it out of the dark and into our cultural conversations about higher education. It's also about dismantling the unrealistic and sometimes toxic expectations we have for ourselves and one another, as well as dismantling the culture that feeds these beliefs. This book is not about a career unraveling; it's about reckoning with ourselves, one another, and the culture of higher education to make it better for colleagues, students, and those academics coming after us.

How Is the Book Organized?

Unraveling Faculty Burnout is unique in structure as well as content. Each chapter includes pieces of my personal burnout story, individual narratives from faculty women, and observations and suggestions from researchers, educational and faculty developers, and coaching professionals about ways to begin to break down a wall for individuals and higher ed culture more broadly. Each chapter is different; some focus more on stories, some have more reflection built in, some have more activities and advice, and some have longer interviews with coaches. But in each chapter you will find multiple ways to think more deeply about the chapter's theme.

The book is organized in two major sections. The first section dives into some of the cultural and personal factors that may contribute to faculty burnout and its related mental health challenges, such as depression and anxiety. Chapter 1 examines the cultural elements implicated in faculty burnout, including the culture of competition and productivity that shames "unproductive" faculty, the scarcity of resources, and continual expectation escalation. The chapter also emphasizes why we need to talk about burnout early and often among ourselves, with our graduate students, and with administration. Chapter 2 explores the academic identities of women in higher education, including the personality traits and thinking patterns that may be common to many of us who chose faculty life, such as perfectionism, overachieving, and imposter syndrome.

The second section introduces four elements for understanding and addressing faculty burnout: purpose, compassion, connection, and balance. In chapter 3, on *purpose*, readers will come to understand the relationship between burnout and one's sense of meaningful work. Chapter 4 explores how we can treat ourselves and those around us with *compassion*. The chapter examines how negative self-talk, compassion fatigue, perceived professional competition, and expectation escalation can present along our vitality journeys and offers strategies for showing self-compassion as well as compassion for others.

In chapter 5, we turn to how to cultivate *connection* to trusted peers, to those we serve and mentor, and to those outside of the university. Connection is an important means of overcoming the shame and isolation of a burnout experience, and this chapter addresses finding your people and supportive others and pursuing outside experiences. Chapter 6, on *balance*, offers more than the trite advice to just get a massage or take a short vacation. While short-term self-care can alleviate symptoms in the moment, burnout runs deeper; this chapter suggests how to pursue personal and professional vitality by setting boundaries, not overidentifying with job as self, and cultivating hobbies and nonacademic pursuits.

Finally, after a brief coda, there are four appendixes, comprising minichapters that appeal directly to faculty and educational developers, two bonus interviews, and a variety of additional exercises to continue building one's self-awareness about burnout, including a set of guided questions and a brief activity for faculty just beginning to question their relationship to work and burnout.

Burnout thrives in the shadows of professional shame. But when we bring it into the light, talk to one another, and drive change, we reclaim our narratives and ourselves. Before we begin, a note.

A Personal Note

This book is not intended to be the definitive research survey of burnout in faculty. Like any book, it's incomplete in a variety of ways. I could have done more research, reviewed more literature, read or reached out directly to more scholars. I wish more men had connected with me to tell their stories. And I deeply wish I could have connected with more women from marginalized populations. This is a book about the stories, the personal, vulnerable, unvarnished sharing of a life experience many of us have but do not speak of. I want the voices to speak for themselves rather than be wrapped up in traditional argumentation. I did my best to honor both the research and the direct experience of the women I spoke with as well as my own. And I chose not to discuss certain situations and conflicts that contributed to the height of my burnout.

I did not write this book for recognition or self-promotion, as I would have pre-burnout. I wrote it because I needed to write it. And the reactions to my story have suggested that many of you need it too. If burnout has taught me anything—and trust me, it has taught me many things, as you will see in these pages—it's that I have emotional, intellectual, and personal limits, and these limits are not weaknesses. It's more that I am human (gasp), and all humans are vulnerable no matter how hard we try to bury our humanity or beat it into submission or publish something so that the experience will have actually "meant something." Burnout has taught me that I am enough, with or without this book.

This book is for me and for you, no matter how human and vulnerable you are right now. I'm not an expert on burnout or a certified or practicing mental health professional. I'm an academic who tapped into some of the more toxic aspects of her personality and the culture of higher ed. After doing so for too long, I crashed hard and had to build myself back up from the ground. It was hard and awful, but I'm still here, and I'm a better version of myself in higher education and a better person than I was before.

This book represents my recovery in so many ways, the lessons I learned and the wisdom of others in higher ed who have experienced burnout. The book is meant to show that you are not alone, burnout isn't necessarily the end of something, and you can move through burnout onto whatever path you choose inside or outside higher ed. But it's hard work, and some elements of the book you may need to linger over or allow yourself to be uncomfortable with. Once that is established, together we can write the next chapter in the stories of burnout in higher education.

Reflection Opportunity

- What attracted you to higher education?
- What were you most passionate about when you began your career in higher ed?
- What accomplishment(s) are you most proud of?
- When do you feel your best at work?
- What values and meaningful goals do you have for your academic career? Do you feel that you are honoring those values and goals currently? Why, or why not?

- Can you identify a specific time when your passion waned? What happened? How did you rebound, or why didn't you rebound?

- What, if any, aspects of your work do you dread? Why? What underlies that dread? What would happen if you eliminated that aspect?

- If you could change anything about your current context, what would it be, and why? If such change magically occurred one night, how would you know it the next day? How would you feel?

CHAPTER 1

Culture

I'm not sure what made me feel more ashamed when I heard my burn-out diagnosis—that I had the holy grail of academic jobs with tenure and was totally miserable or that I was too scared to make a change and potentially leave a profession I was really good at for who knew what. I saw my reputation, everything I had worked so hard to create, shattering because I was not good enough.

After my therapist, Laura, diagnosed my burnout, like any good academic, rather than dealing with the personal toll the word *burnout* was taking on me, I hit the databases, pulling up as much research as I could, mostly in the organizational psychology journals. Maybe I could prove that burnout wasn't the correct preliminary diagnosis, that it was something else, something that wouldn't shatter my career. But as I skimmed through the research and took a free partial version of the Maslach Burnout Inventory, the most validated survey instrument, it was hard to continue to tell myself I wasn't burned out. Clinically, not just situationally. I scored off the charts on the inventory and saw myself reflected in much of the research on healthcare professionals, social workers, and teachers.

In so many ways, admitting I had burnout was shameful to me. I thought I was stronger. How could I be so weak? I asked myself. Those around me were just as busy and stressed, if not more, especially those colleagues I judged myself against, who represented the next bar I had to reach. They seemed to be doing just fine, so why was I different all of the sudden? They clearly liked their students, when I barely tolerated mine. They were writing and presenting, while I was hiding in my house. They were leading meetings, while I was cowering in the stairwell trying to figure out what to eat for lunch. I didn't even have children to worry about or "get in the way" of uninterrupted time to work and produce. If I couldn't achieve or *do* higher ed, who was I? Could I still have a place within the only system I belonged to, or was I weak, useless, dead weight now?

At the time of that first meeting with Laura, I completely believed that admitting I was well and truly burned out would be disastrous for my career, my reputation, and my book sales, given that my book was about faculty productivity and vitality. Higher ed culture told me my worth was based on my productivity; I was only as good as the number of articles I published, the scores I received on my end-of-semester student evaluations, the level at which I could compete with other scholars to increase the reputation of my institution, and the sheer number of hours I dedicated to "doing" higher ed. Being weak or making work for others because you can't handle it any longer—these are things you just don't do if you want to develop or maintain your credibility as a serious academic.

Perhaps the hardest mind-set I had to shift was admitting I was human, not just a professor: I couldn't keep up with the cultural expectation escalation for my career. I struggled to accept that I couldn't write about the design-thinking pilot program because it had deeply scarred me or that I might not write for a long while. I had to acknowledge that the titles, awards, and other recognition I was always striving for were about external validation, not about pursuing a true purpose or passion.

In those early weeks of therapy, and for the first time ever, I started to actively imagine my exit strategy because I knew that I could not continue to function at the same level that I had in the past without hurtling toward a true nervous breakdown. I didn't know how to do this job any other way. I knew I had skills that would translate well into a nonacademic job or into a consulting business should I decide to leave. But could I walk away from what I'd thought until recently was a true calling, especially knowing how difficult it would be to get back in if I changed my mind? If I did walk away, would anyone notice? Or was I what I feared most—replaceable and irrelevant?

If students repeatedly fail your exam, is it the students' fault, for not studying hard enough, or yours? If burnout is running rampant among faculty in US higher ed, are the individuals to blame for not being "strong enough" to survive in academia? Or is the system itself to blame for creating conditions that value productivity and busyness over the whole person? A system that persuades us academia is a higher calling, that we are fortunate to have jobs when so many other smart, capable colleagues are scraping by in precarious adjunct roles, that our identities must revolve around our institutions and disciplines and that leaving high ed is a failure of character.

Over the next few months, I'd come to admit that my entire self-worth was wrapped up in what higher ed culture defined as success: scholarly productivity, awards, teaching evaluations, overcommitment to service at the institution and in disciplinary organizations, and recognition of my accomplishments by those around me. But that was a long, complicated process involving a lot of talking about my feelings, which I apparently do have. It took me two breakdowns, medical leave, years of therapy, and the right combination of medications—and now distance—to get to a place where I can talk openly about my experience with burnout without feeling deep shame.

And the more I opened up, to colleagues and peers, and eventually #AcademicTwitter, the more stories I heard from others, heartbreaking stories of shame, burden, fear, and even nihilism and serious physical and mental health problems. So why do we do it? And more importantly, can we change it?

Reflection Opportunity

Zaynab Sabagh, Nathan Hall, and Alenoush Saroyan (2018) distill a large body of literature to enumerate indicators of occupational well-being, including job satisfaction, quitting intentions, job involvement, engagement, organizational commitment, and organizational citizenship behaviors, as well as stress, health problems, anxiety, and psychological complaints (141). Before reading on, take time to reflect on where you stand with regard to the indicators that resonate most with you. In what areas is the culture of your institution healthy and encouraging? Where does it fall short, and how does that impact faculty well-being and burnout?

Hiding in Plain Sight

I've publicly written about burnout, and since the pandemic I've led what feels like countless burnout-resilience workshops for institutions ranging from small privates to huge R1 institutions, even an Ivy. I always start these workshops the same way, with a few questions. After giving the participants time before we start to jot down some thoughts about what they give themselves permission to do or not do, say or not say, during our hour together, I ask them to add to the chat their favorite things about working with their colleagues and students. Answers are usually similar—smart colleagues who care about students, students actively engaged in classes, the joy of big ideas, and seeing realization dawn on students' faces. No one ever says meetings or grading or bureaucracy.

The second question I ask is, "How are you doing, really?" I have them take the much-abbreviated version of the Maslach Burnout Inventory and rate themselves for each question along a scale of 1 (never) to 5 (very often) (see appendix 2 for the full exercise). They then input their most common score—mostly 3s or mostly 5s, for example—into an anonymous Google poll that lets us see the results in a real-time pie chart. The number of attendees at these workshops ranges from twenty to fifty, but the results are pretty consistent: half of the people rate themselves as mostly 3s, or "at risk." Maybe one or two people rate themselves in the "no danger" category, and there are always a few in the "danger" zone of mostly 5s. The remaining 25 percent fall into the "at some risk" and "at serious risk" categories.

Then I ask participants to interpret the results, nonstatistical as the results may be. Again, I hear the same things: "some of our colleagues are in serious distress" and "at least 60 percent of our colleagues feel some significant danger of burnout." Someone invariably comments that they "thought there would be more 5s," to which someone else always responds that "people who most need a workshop on burnout can't or won't attend." The reasons given for the latter's nonattendance vary: not knowing they are in burnout danger; not being emotionally ready to talk about or hear about it; or just being plain scared of outing themselves as "a burnout." And some notice that the vast majority of the workshop attendees are usually women.

For many, this is the first time they have thought seriously about burnout in themselves and possibly their colleagues and what it means to be burned out. Higher ed is not a culture that is kind to perceived weakness in faculty, whether we like to admit it or not. And burnout can look like weakness—the exhaustion, the pushing away, the thoughts that nothing we do has any meaning. I could spend years trying to make this argument, but other have already taken up that charge. In this chapter I focus on a few aspects of our culture that foment burnout. I zero in on academic capitalism specifically and the ways it breeds elements ground in emotional and hope labor, exploitation, and competition.

But I don't claim that higher ed culture is only bad or destructive. Higher education at its best is a haven for intellectual exploration, lifelong learning, and civic optimism. Higher ed can nurture creativity, inspire innovation, and connect people in indelible ways. I have collaborated with enthusiastic colleagues on research and teaching, been awed by the ingenuity of my students' work in our communities, and served with peers and administrators who truly believe in higher education's potential to foster students' intellectual, social, and civic growth. Before burnout, I believed this too. But the burnout took over, and I was at my most cynical, seeing only capitalism, exploitation, and competition.* I'm still working back from that.

Playing the Market

For most of my academic career and life, I was obsessed with productivity. I wasn't what elite higher ed would call prolific, but I was productive for my corner of academia. Productivity was a way I judged myself—in papers written and published, conference acceptances, positive course evaluations, student fellows and undergraduate researchers advised,

---

* Yes, that's a bit dramatic, but burnout does that to you. Emotions feel both dulled and heightened at the same time, which makes it difficult to function in the system spawning them.

and leadership roles earned.* When I was productive, I had something tangible to prove my worth—look how much I'm writing, teaching, advising. See? I deserve to be here. It wasn't until I was deep into therapy for burnout that I realized that the culture of academia is one of supply and demand, product and service, faculty as cogs in the machine.

I get very mixed reactions when I express my post-burnout belief that working in higher ed is just a job in an industry like any other job in an industry. Yes, faculty are highly trained scholars, teachers,† and researchers, but in the end higher ed is increasingly driven by the need to generate income. Some people tell me they find relief in thinking about what they do as a job; others push back or leave the conversation entirely because to them academia is a higher calling, one that few can answer, and they believe that those who can should dedicate their all. I would argue that faculty work can be both job and calling, but as universities become more administration heavy, driven more by grants and profit, and more exploitative of faculty labor and productivity, the more we lean into academic capitalism and a student-as-customer mentality.

This move away from generating knowledge and learning and into the market is partially a product of precipitous decline in government spending on public higher education and the neoliberal mentality in society at large. As institutions and faculty become more dependent on outside funding, competition for that money grows, and market-driven economics reign; institutions actively seek profit-generating opportunities through "endowment funds, university-industry partnerships, institutional investment in professors' spinoff companies, and an increase in student tuition and fees" (Jessop 2018; Koenig 2019;

---

* I also created roles for myself and craftily persuaded people to let me develop something or run something else.
† Sometimes. Training faculty to teach, and not just to do research, is woefully behind in higher education.

Padilla and Thompson 2016; Park 2011, 87). As they do so, authority gravitates to those generating revenue, very often away from the core mission of educating students, which is typically done by women, people of color, and contingent faculty (Koenig 2019, 3).

When this already elitist and patriarchal culture shifts to a model of efficiency, faculty are expected to do more with less, which can lead to an increase in burnout on campus, and an institution can justify exploitations like that of adjunct faculty (Billot 2010; Clegg 2008; Padilla and Thompson 2016; Winter 2009). The experience of a non-tenure-track faculty member, Candace, illustrates the damage that can result.

> When I accepted a position as a full-time non-tenure-track (NTT) faculty member, I was elated. I was an experienced college teacher with years of classroom experience as an adjunct. I was ready to settle in, join the academic community, and contribute to student success. I believed—and still believe—in the importance of teaching and have dedicated my career to making others successful. In that sense, I was an ideal NTT faculty member, as I was capable and willing to work hard, with a deep commitment to students. I joined a small group of dedicated college teachers, almost all of them women, who were excited to do the same. I knew our role on campus would be different than that of the tenured and tenure-track faculty, but I naively expected our work to be valued equally in a university setting.
>
> Like most NTT positions, mine came with a heavy teaching load and high expectations for student involvement. Within my first two years, I took on additional responsibilities, led projects, designed a research forum for early undergraduates, and began designing activities tied to our university's strategic goals and assessment of learning results. I advised two student organizations and

sat on university committees. I acted as an academic adviser and supported students. My days were filled with activity, and I took pride in my work. I was typical of my NTT colleagues, active and student-focused with high energy and productivity.

Unfortunately, the campus community did not embrace a new class of faculty on campus. Senior faculty were suspicious of what they considered administrative faculty and spoke negatively about us. The most upsetting conversation I had, though, was with an administrator from my department. She made a point of telling me not to plan for the future, as I was temporary. She stated that that the university planned to use contingent faculty as heavily as possible, burning them out and then replacing them.

When I realized that I was a disposable faculty member, my view of myself and my position changed. Even as tenured faculty began to accept the NTT faculty, the administration became more consistent in reminding the campus that we were contingent. As I became more active in the broader academic world, I realized this idea was echoed in institutions throughout the country. While not all institutions were as strident or utilitarian as my own, the underlying message was the same: NTT faculty were contingent and therefore not valued or viewed as long-term members of the campus community.

Over the years, even as course loads became heavier, administrative duties were added to the position. As the days became busier and the list of tasks grew, I moved course planning and student feedback to evenings and weekends. I felt overwhelmed by the sheer amount of work, and with the echo of "disposable faculty" in mind, my feeling of being overwhelmed turned to anxiety. But in many ways I was more productive and creative than ever, teaching, writing, mentoring faculty, and advising students. My days were full, and I rarely had time for reflection.

Before I experienced it, I thought faculty who were burned out were no longer capable of teaching. They were people who had lost interest in students and the classroom and instead went through the motions without investment. I pictured people who had lost all vibrance and who were in some indescribable way faded copies of who they had once been. I, on the other hand, had retreated to the classroom, viewing it as a place where I was successful and needed. I did not recognize the signs of burnout in myself and never considered that the energy I felt might be fueled by anxiety. I was usually able to redirect it into productivity and creativity, especially in the classroom, but it came at a cost. I still find myself wondering what I might have achieved if I had been given the opportunity to reflect and work from passion and interest rather than fear and economics.

Candace's story is not uncommon among contingent and NTT faculty I spoke with; teaching was a labor of love that could be exploited. With her story in mind, two additional sources forwarded my thinking about the idea that one must act on a calling to be successful in higher ed, which often means giving exponentially more than one gets back: Kelly J. Baker's *Grace Period: A Memoir in Pieces* (2017) and Sarah Jaffe's *Work Won't Love You Back: How Devotion to Our Jobs Keeps Us Exploited, Exhausted, and Alone* (2021). Although our experiences in higher ed differed, Baker's thoughts on loving academic work to one's personal and professional detriment deeply resonated with my own experience. She writes that

academic love is inherently one-sided. I could love my field without reservation, but the field could never really love me back. That's the danger of investing wholeheartedly in any work; the return never matches the devotion. This love is sacrificial and rarely redemptive. The price it extracts is too high. It breaks our hearts into sharp, pained pieces. Love, like optimism, can turn cruel. . . . And here's the problem: Exploitation doesn't make us love our work less. Instead, it often pushes us to love that work more—to consider it something deeper, a vocation instead of just a job. I clung more tightly to academic love at the low points of my career, as if all I needed was love to remedy my situation. (29–30)

Jaffe's discussion of the labor of love myth in both K–12 and higher education mirrors Candace's and Baker's personal experiences, claiming that the anachronistic structure of the academy relies on creating and maintaining hope labor among optimistic grad students and faculty:

This hierarchy is justified as paying one's dues, but it also, importantly, functions to maintain quality control. Not just anyone can be a professor; one must have done research judged to count by one's peers, passed through hurdles set by accomplished mentors, smiled through the long hours, and pretended to be cheerful while eating ramen noodles, all this hope labor performed in what used to be more than a hope of a career. Passing through the set of qualifications to a good job at the end was, for a time, a ritual one could more or less count on. Nowadays, this isn't true. (249)

I quote Candace, Baker, and Jaffe at length because their descriptions of the labors of love and hope baked into higher ed illuminate the mental and emotional struggle I and many others have experienced in our burnout. The cultural expectations are set high when we are willing to work from love and hope without recognizing the machine behind that work. And in this culture, it's often women and people of color who are impacted the most. Marie Moeller and Lindsay Steiner shared their wish list for a better culture:

As two now-tenured female-identifying faculty in a large department at a comprehensive institution with shrinking enrollments (except in some specialty areas), we offer five reflections about what we wish we had experienced. We wish for others to experience better than what we did, and we are focused on how we might be able to influence future generations of female-identifying, marginalized, multiply marginalized, and early-career instructors in high-demand, high-yield, high-service expectation fields.

We wish we had experienced a stronger culture of listening. So often in departments, a small number of faculty do the brunt of the service, teaching, and other work that sustains high-demand programs. Yet, such faculty are rarely heard. In other words, privilege begets privilege. Attending to the loudest voices means accepting and perpetuating the status quo. In that model, workload can double for faculty already experiencing expectation escalation. In these moments, we wish leadership had listened more closely. Welcoming everyone into a conversation about addressing burnout and inequitable workload issues can go a long way toward equitable workload assessments, meeting departmental needs, being responsive to student need and demand, understanding staffing affordances and constraints, and providing more specific information for best possible decision making in the department, among other positive effects.

We wish that expertise had been recognized and respected. We live in a culture of the anti-expert; this culture has permeated work at our institution. In our experience, staffing specialization-focused courses with individuals who do not have credentials in the specialization leads to burnout and low faculty morale. For example, while it may be a short-term solution to staffing crises, this practice has long-term impacts on program integrity, advising, recruitment, and retention. This dynamic also creates a pattern of expectation on the part of nonspecialists that anyone can teach specialist courses. Such a practice diminishes the work and disciplinary expertise not only of faculty but of higher education as a whole.

We wish our leadership and department had been more data driven and informed. Reading data honestly and reporting it with transparency can go a long way in supporting faculty. Not doing so gaslights faculty who support and grow programs despite challenges; again, this practice supports a status-quo approach to long-term departmental growth (or lack thereof). Regardless of intent, to faculty lack of transparency can seem intentional and ultimately contribute to low morale and burnout. All faculty must have access to the gamut of variables that surround workload equity, hiring practices, budgetary decisions, and other key aspects of program and curriculum management.

We wish workload inequity had been addressed more overtly. Institutions tend to remove or sequester individuals who do not, or choose not to, excel in particular at service and teaching. Such workload reassignment, however, is not substituted for equitable work but often occurs as research reassignment for that individual. This practice rewards individuals for not being team players. We wish that more of our leaders had recognized and addressed workload inequity in ways that did not reward mediocrity. We encourage writing bylaws with explicit service expectations, with the consequence of poor performance being the requirement to serve the university in another capacity.

We wish we had experienced a collaborative instead of a competitive department. We wish that faculty from other disciplines in the same department would have championed areas besides their own. This would have showed us that faculty were aware of other programs in the department, could speak to the issues they faced, and ultimately could build a team of faculty in the department who respected one another's work and programs.

Calling Out Culture

The challenges and exploitation of women, especially women of color, in higher ed are no secret. Women face all manner of explicit and implicit biases, from sexism and sexual harassment to motherhood taxes with respect to maternity leave and childcare, unfair teaching evaluations, unbalanced service loads and emotional labor, and well-known disparities in salary compared with men faculty (Cardel et al. 2020). Higher ed is also a place where a display of emotions is often unwelcome and may be seen as weak or unbecoming of a serious scholar (Stupnisky, Hall, and Pekrun 2019a, 1495). And Amado Padilla (1994, 26) calls out the cultural taxation placed on women faculty of color especially when called upon to serve as representative multicultural members of committees to show their "good citizenship."

The academic and coach Michelle Dionne Thompson works with early-career women faculty of color who are experiencing these biases.

> For women and people of color, and women of color in particular, to niche down even more, a capitalistic system needs successes in order to say, "See, it works." For example, I got my doctorate in history from NYU. The first Black person to graduate from the history program with a PhD did so, I think, in 2006. One thinks of how long this institution has been around, and you have to believe that history was probably

one of the fundamental departments. But 2006 being the first year a Black person received a doctorate? I've seen some of my fellow graduates thrive, but there are many whom I've never seen again.

In this workplace culture it's hard when women don't get mentored and people of color don't get mentored. Within higher ed institutions, that only contributes to the challenges of burnout, right? Where do you go to ask questions about this? What do I mean by "the culture"? Why are they saying that to me? Why does this work the way it does? Why is it that when I talk to clients and ask what they need to get tenure, they don't know?

In 2020, we still don't have these answers, and you expect women and people of color to thrive in this context? It's not impossible, but sometimes it's untenable. I know that white male faculty will reach out to fellow white male faculty, inviting them to dinner and sharing what they did with their time and how to succeed. White men have access to these informal networks. No one hides the ball from them, but everyone else has to work themselves into the ground, so of course they're going to burn out because they don't know what's expected of them.

I do a lot of burnout prevention work because I can't stand to see this industry eat up people, really brilliant women and women of color, in the way that it has. I can't stand watching it.

None of these challenges are new or, unfortunately, surprising, but they do still directly impact job satisfaction, retention, and promotion for women faculty. I've also heard disturbing stories of bullying and harassment that the culture of individual institutions allowed to persist even after they were reported. For example, an assistant professor at a rural state institution told me she had taken the job, in a location and role she would not have considered, just to get away from the bullying and gaslighting at her previous institution, which ultimately had impacted her health and mental well-being:

> I had been excited to enter my graduate program. I was ready to work hard, impress my faculty members, and make some new friends and colleagues. That lasted about a year, until I realized just how badly I was being manipulated by some of my peers. They would distort my words about the program or other grad students and treat me as if I were either invisible or idiotic in classes, while the faculty member did nothing to stop it. Once, I went to a professor in one of the courses in which the bullying was happening, and she basically told me that it happens and to toughen up. I started developing nervous habits, picking my eyebrows, but I was determined to show them I was capable and smart. Even as I tried, the bullying continued.
>
> I finished the program by sheer force of will, but the burnout and mental anguish have stuck with me. I took the first job I was offered. It's not a place my partner and I want to be, but it got me as far away from my graduate school as possible at the time. In many ways, the job itself is good, but I'm exhausted all the time, can't bond with my department because I'm overly cautious, and regularly wonder why I'm still in academia at all. I guess we'll see.

And several women told me the all too common story of being sexually harassed by male colleagues or others in the institutional "family." A dear friend told me that she had been harassed and nearly assaulted by a university board member at her prestigious institution:

> He was a familiar face on campus, well connected and generally liked by everyone. As a board member, he was progressive and seemed really concerned with making sure students received an excellent education. He

was also really wealthy, and people tripped over themselves to keep him happy. It wasn't unusual for him to invite faculty members to lunch or happy hour to talk about their programs and goals. Looking back now, I can see how weird that was. When he invited me, I thought he wanted to talk about the new service-learning initiative I had started. He didn't.

I met him at his on-campus "office" to talk, but it quickly became clear he wanted something else from me. I kept trying to turn the conversation back to the institution and the program, but he didn't care. When I said no in no uncertain terms, he started yelling at me, calling me terrible names, and making gross sexual remarks. I left shaking.

Of course, I reported him to my chair and to HR. I filed the appropriate grievance form, but all I got was a runaround for weeks until someone eventually told me that nothing was going to happen so I should just move on. I couldn't believe the institution that I had loved so much would protect a donor over a faculty member. I left as soon as I could, despite being a full professor, because I couldn't stay there. It was just the last straw in a long series of events. And now I'm trying to rebuild a career. I'm exhausted and hurt.

How many other stories have we not heard or listened too? The system is just as complicit here as the bullies and harassers.

In some ways, "doing" higher ed is a performance of idealistic views of what it means to be an academic. But eventually you realize that whatever you can do in teaching, research, and service will never be enough, no matter how much of yourself and your well-being you give (Knights and Clarke 2014, 338; Thomason 2012, 30). Faculty participants in a study by David Knights and Caroline Clarke called academia a "treadmill" on which you have to always "be excellent" because "the job is never done; it's never done properly, and it's never done well enough. You're always feeling terribly guilty" (339–44). This level of conflict between culture and expectations, on the one hand, and a sense of belonging and fulfilment, on the other, contributes to burnout (Sabagh, Hall, and Saroyan 2018, 132). And that conflict creates a culture that is often isolating and competitive.

Competing to Connect

Thinking about higher ed culture as capitalist and driven by competition, I can admit that I have always had a nemesis. They never knew I thought of them as such, but at every stage of my pre-burnout life there was someone I felt a deep need to compare myself with and be better than. In grade school it was a boy named Jerry. Every nine weeks, when our teachers put our honor-roll GPAs on the blackboard, I would internally gloat or chastise myself depending on how I measured up. In college it was my boyfriend*; in grad school, the person with better design skills. In academia it was the peer who landed a role on an executive committee before I did; at work, it was a colleague who was always three steps ahead of me. These were not exactly healthy fixations. When I could not measure up, I internalized shame; in some cases, I allowed myself to be bullied and gaslit as I put everything I had into being better than.

While I've cynically come to think of the narrative of work as home and colleagues as family as capitalistic and exploitative, I did have supportive colleagues who were constants in my professional life, and we went through many things together. And yet I still hid my burnout as long as possible, knowing deep down that it was not safe to share with certain people. I may have been catastrophizing, but I believed there were those who would use my burnout against me, those for whom I had

---

* This happened in several cases, and yes, it was unhealthy for these relationships. I didn't know how not to compare myself with them and believed I needed a leg up to be an equal in the relationships.

never been good enough even before burnout. I knew subconsciously that opening the door to what I was feeling would force me to admit to being used in some cases and that returning to that environment after medical leave would be impossible.

Ann Austin (2002) argues that the depth and breadth of entrenched higher ed culture have an impact whether or not institutional faculty are supportive and generous toward one another or aggressive and competitive (in Lumpkin 2014, 198). Miguel Padilla and Julia Thompson (2016) found peer support to be one of the most important factors in mitigating burnout, saying that strong social support and clear job expectations lead to less of a likelihood of burnout (557). And Knights and Clarke (2014) summarize multiple studies, finding higher ed a place where "competitiveness, intellectualism, achievement-orientation, hierarchy, and evaluativeness [may give rise to] all manner of high emotions, anxieties, defenses, denials, deceptions and self-deceptions, rivalries, insecurities, threats, vulnerabilities, [and] intimacies" (338).

Bullying and gaslighting can be masked as mentoring and support, which contributes to imposter syndrome, levels of intimidation, feelings of not being "enough" in one's work, and ultimately isolation, all driven by external voices that lead to shame and vulnerability, as the coach Katie Linder described to me:

Thinking about the values of higher ed . . . Definitely process, lifelong learning, loyalty, growth. But, also, competition and productivity. And there's definitely a value in there of insecurity and benefiting from other people's insecurity, which when you put it out there is just awful. But it is definitely a hallmark of higher ed. Every academic I've worked with has imposter syndrome to some degree, and I feel like it's almost trained into us in graduate school, where there's just no affirmation. You're constantly being questioned. The tacit knowledge is not shared in a way that you feel like you will ever understand it. So yeah, it's hard, but that's happening in higher education. And how we abuse the adjunct system—it's really built on insecurity and exploitation.

Ilana felt much of this pressure and isolation as a graduate student and later as a person with burnout who took a break before looking for academic jobs:

> A big part of what was so hard about graduate school and what can be so hard about departmental life is a sense of isolation. It's just a very alienating experience, and there's this very strong sense of competition. Even a couple of years ago, I had a conversation with my dissertation adviser. I had a vague idea of what I should be doing in terms of applying for postdocs and tenure-track jobs and stuff like that, but not really a clear plan, since I'd taken a break from academia after completing my PhD due to burnout. I think I was just so exhausted at the thought of going back the way I was "supposed to." My adviser said, "Well, now, you've been out three years, and everybody else has been publishing." Not in a mean way, but reminding me that I've fallen behind. It's this unending sense of pressure and competition, and there aren't enough jobs, and there are so many candidates, and they're so brilliant. It's just the sense that if you let your guard down for a moment, you fall behind and can never catch up. I think that's just the pervasive culture. In a way, he was right because I'm still working as an adjunct, so half in and half out of higher ed.

Ilana missed a sense of social support and positive connection to others that would have positively impacted her ability to thrive in graduate school and beyond. Andrea, an NTT faculty member on a yearly contract, experienced bias and lack of support among her tenure-track and tenured colleagues, which contributed to her experience with burnout:

I'm still experiencing the lack of support from tenure-track faculty and the lack of recognition of my successes. And that's not just me; there's such a big separation between tenured faculty and our non-tenured research group even though we do the same amount of work, the same type of work that tenure-track folks do. I would often find myself being asked to explain to tenure-track faculty what I do and why I could say some things but not others in departmental meetings. I had to stay quiet because my contract was on an annual basis.

So even the most progressive tenure-track faculty, even the ones that you would think would not be "fake liberals," the ones who really were thinking about equality, failed to see the power differential between tenure-track and non-tenure-track faculty and put a lot of weight on our shoulders too. We are the ones that are doing all the undergrad recruitment events. We're the ones that go to the Senate or whatever it is because tenure-track faculty have "other responsibilities." Between the extra work and the fact that that work is not recognized and you're actually being blamed for some of your situation, you're like, Oh, I just can't. That contributed a lot to the burnout. I kept thinking, how do I make them see what we do? At least I have my research-center colleagues, all women, who can support and encourage me when I'm down or frustrated.

Both Ilana and Andrea found collegial support and positive interactions to be absent from their work, either partially or entirely, and burnout research done by Maslach, Schaufeli, and Leiter (2001) shows that a sense of thriving at work is created when workers "share praise, comfort, happiness, and humor with people they like and respect" that "reaffirms a person's membership in a group with a shared sense of values" (415). But what does that look like in the capitalistic culture of higher ed?

Finding the Way Through

My mission to bring burnout out of the shadows in higher ed and remove its "dirty secret" stigma has been grounded in one thought: *We have to normalize talking about burnout without normalizing the culture that causes it.* Individual interventions help us avoid or deal with burnout, but burnout is a workplace-culture issue, a social issue. Changing culture is a massive undertaking, especially in higher ed, which in many ways has calcified around a culture that benefits from workplace competition, hope labor, inequity, and even shame.

Every time an article about faculty burnout hits the higher ed press, I have two reactions. First, I'm deeply relieved (again) that I am not alone and that others are talking publicly about their experiences. But second, I experience a mishmash of sadness, weariness, and even anger that yet another article about burnout needed to be published. And while before the pandemic of 2020 there were only occasional articles about burnout, it became one of the most talked about issues in the *Chronicle* and *Inside Higher Ed* during the pandemic.

I'm grateful for the courage colleagues have shown by sharing their stories, complete with individual steps to take in the face of a burnout episode, so that their experiences might be cautionary or inspirational tales for other faculty. But I'm also frustrated that these articles continue to be necessary and focus on tips for individuals rather than calls for systemic change, my own articles and podcast guest spots included.

We can pretend that the system isn't to blame or that we don't all play a role in perpetuating it. We are our institutions and culture. What will it take to change this culture from one of productivity and "never enough" to one of care? What we model for our students, both those who might follow in our academic footsteps and those who might not, directly impacts their future. Sometimes I think that by dwelling on faculty burnout I am just drawing attention to a first-world problem, but is that me or higher ed talking? As a colleague reminded me, this may be a first-world problem in a privileged space, but we teach, care for, and mentor our students, who are indeed the future of our society. And they have so much to deal with given the planetary and social legacy we will hand off to them that it is our responsibility to prepare them to be empathetic, resilient, creative, and community-oriented.

Esteve Corbera and colleagues (2020) offer a call for the academy to rethink practices in the pandemic that sums up our charge to change the higher ed culture that causes burnout in the first place:

> We advocate for prioritizing collective rather than individual goals, whilst remaining accountable to our universities and being scientifically responsive. This means paying attention to teaching, mentoring, and supporting students; (re)designing research projects in ways that are more socially meaningful, environmentally sustainable, and less stressful for those involved; and contributing to institutional initiatives aimed at fostering collegiality and collective support. (193)

What would happen if we took advantage of the moment in the aftermath of the COVID-19 pandemic to change the culture, not just address burnout in individual cases? Work environments and cultures cause burnout, and addressing the problem only at the level of the individual faculty member ignores or avoids the systemic causes of burnout (Maslach, Schaufeli, and Leiter 2001, 419). What if addressing the inequalities experienced by women, faculty of color, and other marginalized groups led to an increased attention to implicit and explicit bias, mental health and well-being, competition culture, bullying, and forms of exploitation at play in the culture (Young 2020)?

What would higher ed culture look like if we heeded this call? I think we can be more purpose-driven, compassionate, connected, and balanced.

Reflection Opportunity

Return to your reflection from the beginning of the chapter and recall Sabagh, Hall, and Saroyan's (2018) indicators of occupational well-being: job satisfaction, quitting intentions, job involvement, engagement, organizational commitment, and organizational citizenship behaviors, as well as stress, health problems, anxiety, and psychological complaints (141). Now that you've read the chapter, do the same the indicators still resonate most with you? In what areas of your institution is the culture healthy and encouraging? Where does it fall short, and how does that impact faculty well-being and burnout?

Are there ways to improve the culture? That is a theme you'll see throughout this book. While the majority of interventions for burnout are individual, we have to change the culture underneath to really see shifts.

* * * CHAPTER BONUS * * *
Doing Nothing as Capitalist Intervention
JENNIFER MARLOW

When I was a child, one of my favorite books was Leo Lionni's *Frederick* (1967). Frederick is a field mouse who lives in a grey stone wall with his extended family. As the summer ends, the other field mice busily prepare for the long winter ahead by foraging for provisions and carrying them into their abode. In contrast, Frederick sits quietly atop the stone wall, eyes half-closed. His fellow field mice are angry and resentful as they work hard and Frederick sits there seemingly doing nothing. It turns out, however, that Frederick was storing up the warm rays of the sun, absorbing the bright colors of his surroundings, and composing poetry and stories in his head to share with all the mice during the winter.

Even as a young child, I felt sharply judgmental of Frederick. As much as I loved the scene of the hollow in the stone wall, warm and glowing as a result of Frederick's work, I somehow intuitively knew that Frederick still didn't quite fit in. Before I even began to experience work myself, I saw Frederick as a kind of hero, but a kind that I would never be.

Frederick has never left me. Four decades later, I am an associate professor of English at a small, private liberal-arts college. And despite being midcareer, having secured tenure and promotion, I never feel free of the pressures of higher education—pressures that have only increased with the corporatization of higher education.

This corporatization is nothing new. An abundance of books and articles have been written on the subject over the past two decades (see Aronowitz 2000; Bousquet 2008; Giroux 2002, 2003; and Readings 1996). However, it's not just the corporate takeover of our campus eateries and bookstores, the private money funding research studies, and the administrative bloat that are making higher education increasingly corporate. It is also the way many faculty are being asked to do more with less: retain students, assess and assess our assessments, create ready-to-use online curriculums, write more reports, serve on more committees. We are given paper-pushing work that used to be the purview of administrators but no longer is despite their increased numbers. And then there are the age-old characteristics of life in academia—the rat-race mentality, the pressure to "publish or perish"—only made worse by a shrinking job market and school closures. Academia has long been competitive, but that competitiveness has only increased under late-stage capitalism.

My reckoning with burnout came, unironically, at an academic conference. I had risen early and run on the treadmill in the hotel's tiny, dark ill-equipped exercise room along with three women whom I recognized as conference attendees. I had then showered, FaceTimed with my wife and son, and made my way down to breakfast. Having presented the day before, my chest felt marginally lighter without the pressure of a presentation ahead of me that day, but I was also weighed down by considerations of trying to leave my area of specialization (computers and writing). I felt that my field, which is focused on rapidly changing technologies, was simply moving too quickly for me. I needed a way out. As I sat there, scrolling through news articles on my phone, I happened upon Anne Helen Petersen's *Buzzfeed News* article, "How Millennials Became the Burnout Generation." I read it in deep gulps and had an "a-ha-duh moment": I was burnt out.

While not a millennial myself, I felt as if I had received an accurate diagnosis after a long period of not knowing what was wrong. I had been so eager to find a reason for, and to fix, my feelings of being overwhelmed and exhausted that I had blamed my field. But Petersen's article provided me with a more likely culprit: the corporate university.

As with any diagnosis though, treatment is key. Short of revolution (attempting to overthrow the system often leads to more intense burnout), how does one continue to live and work in a corporatized structure and avoid burnout?

On this same conference trip, I purchased a copy of Jenny Odell's book *How to Do Nothing: Resisting the Attention Economy* (2019). Reading it on the plane ride home, I was inspired by Odell's Thoreau-style call to resistance through the seemingly simple act of doing nothing. However, doing nothing is actually far from simple. Odell opens the book with stories of people sitting quietly doing nothing in their work-place cafeteria, or even worse, slowly wandering around the workplace with a vacant look in their eyes. These people were judged by colleagues as strange and potentially lazy. They were the contemporary, human version of Frederick sitting alone atop the stone wall.

Despite its title, Odell's book doesn't actually tell you how to do nothing. Instead, it's a philosophical call not to perform as expected in a capitalist economy within which our attention is a highly sought-after labor and commodity. Attention, while it might not feel like "work," is a form of labor. It takes energy. It is human action in the ex-ternal world that takes exertion on the part of our brains. Social media, advertising, websites—all of these forms of media are designed to cap-ture our attention, which is then turned into a saleable commodity. If you want to overthrow the system, withhold labor, withhold buying power. Marxism 101. However, Odell's call isn't for picket lines or boycotts; it's for "doing nothing," or as she terms it, "resistance-in-place" (xvi).

> To resist in place is to make oneself into a shape that cannot so easily be appropriated by a capitalist value system. To do this means refusing the frame of reference: in this case, a frame of reference in which value is defined by productivity, the strength of one's career, and individual en-trepreneurship. . . . In an environment completely geared toward capi-talist appropriation of even our smallest thoughts, doing this isn't any less uncomfortable than wearing the wrong outfit to a place with a dress code. . . . Doing nothing is hard. (xvi–xvii)

To say that doing nothing is hard might even be an understatement for those of us in academe. After all, I sit here writing this with the hope that it will be published in a collection, become a line on my CV, and help me get promoted. I sit here writing this while tracking my word count, which I record in a spreadsheet each day. Doing nothing in academe is more than hard. It feels antithetical to the way we were trained, and so, it feels counterintuitive—as if we have to fight back against the core of who we are. I always knew I wouldn't be Frederick.

Here I am, however, decades later and post-tenure, feeling old and frazzled at an academic conference and reading about how to do "nothing" on an airplane, and Odell has persuaded me that this refusal of the "frame of reference," this "resistance-in-place" and "standing apart," is crucial not just to my own well-being but to the well-being of the world.

Odell is also careful not to ground her ideas in a full-on Thoreauvian escape from life. As much as she'd like to live in the woods without a working phone and no access to newspapers, "total renunciation would be a mistake. . . . The world needs my participation more than ever" (61). She doesn't expect any of us to fully disengage. In fact, she expects completely the opposite. She argues that engagement is more necessary than ever.

CHAPTER 2

Academic Identity

I've responded to many different versions of my name over the years. Growing up, I was Becki, so some members of my family and old friends still call me that. When I moved to California after completing my MA in professional writing, I started going by Becca, which seemed more mature to me and had been a name my mom used for me anyway. As I started to publish after completing my PhD, I used my full name, and some colleagues do call me Rebecca. But to my students for my twelve years as a professor I was RPR. I had been signing my emails with my initials, as my father did, and early in my career students just started calling me that. It was better than them misspelling my last name in increasingly more creative ways, so RPR stuck. The nickname caught on in other areas of my life, so friends and colleagues often call me RPR as well.

I've realized in therapy that RPR and Becca are pretty separate people. Looking back, I would often joke on social media at the end of each academic year that RPR was going to hibernate while Becca took over for the summer. Now I can see that for what it was: a ritual dropping of armor I wore every academic year, of a skin I could only shed in private or during sanctioned work breaks. And I vividly remember being depressed for at least a month every summer after submitting grades because no one needed RPR.

RPR was that somewhat intimidating academic whose bitchy resting face could scare the most self-assured students when she chooses to turn it on. If you were her student, you knew that she expected a lot of you, but eventually you realized that she fully believed you could meet those expectations with her support. RPR writes and publishes regularly; she's got books with prestigious presses. She creates projects that will bring her recognition and awards (some of which she urged organizations to create just so she could win them). She is an expert in project management, having written the faculty-development book adapting Scrum for academics; and she's on top of everything. She always steps up and into leadership roles. She's not afraid to express unpopular opinions, which she sometimes does a little more sarcastically than necessary. She will call you on your bullshit. She can be a badass.

We all have those different sides of ourselves. But RPR was a persona I created that totally took over my life. The more stressed out I became, the harder I leaned into RPR. The farther I spiraled into burnout, the more I desperately tried to cling to that persona, not realizing that it was the very thing weighing me down. Armor is heavy. If I'm totally honest, the seeds of RPR were planted in elementary school, as the typical smart, socially awkward kid who builds an identity in her intelligence. One who measured her relative worth in comparison with the other smart kids and built a life trying to be better, smarter, more accomplished. That might sound familiar to you.

Higher ed rewards people like RPR. But I wonder how many of those people are wearing armor as I did. I see academics berating their students on Twitter or writing op-eds in the *Chronicle* belittling faculty who show students their vulnerability in Zoom classes necessitated by

COVID-19. I wonder just how burned out those folks are. Do they realize that cynicism and disdain directed at students is a classic sign of burnout? Would they listen to me if I pointed it out? These faculty could very well just be assholes; I'm not dismissing the possibility or even likelihood. But by the time I was barely getting out of bed and putting on my RPR armor, I was an asshole. I was cynical, disdainful, egotistical, and self-important, which kept me from looking at myself and recognizing my own deep unhappiness in my life and career. Everything was blurry—my identity, my thoughts, my future.

RPR was special; Becca was weak and to be hidden. What kind of future could I have when RPR couldn't *do* anything anymore? Of course, I can do things, but I can't do the things I used to do and should be able to do, like write, make it through a departmental meeting without lashing out or having a panic attack, or actually be in my office for more than five minutes before feeling an overwhelming desire to run so no one sees me.

After the breakdown and in therapy, I eventually recognized that I was mourning, which impacted me personally and professionally. I was grieving for the RPR I used to be but would never be again. It took a year of therapy, and a daily struggle to be compassionate toward myself, to see RPR for what she was and to see who I thought Becca was. I needed to integrate those identities in order to move on. I'm grateful for RPR and Becca, but I'm much happier and more content as Rebecca, maybe more so because of the hard, hard work it took to get there.

Reflection Opportunity

- Who are you when you step on campus? stand in front of your class? give a research presentation? Who are you when you aren't doing these things?

- What does being content mean to you? What does it feel like? What impacts might imposter syndrome or perfectionism be having on your ability to be content?
- What measures of success are there besides accomplishments?

Note about Identity

In this chapter I focus on academic identity specifically and draw attention to the roles of imposter syndrome and perfectionism in that identity work. I am not ignoring or diminishing the larger discussions about identity or intersectionality by framing the chapter this way. As I mentioned in the introduction, the majority of contributors and interviewees were white women, though I worked to be more inclusive. The coaches Fatimah Williams and Jane Jones offer some insight into why this might be. Williams notes,

> I'm concerned about how scholars who are women of color understand and measure burnout for themselves, especially against the narrowly defined metrics of recognition and reward that largely overlook their unique experiences in and contributions to the academy. The burden is heavy to constantly navigate these unique demands on top of the pressures of scholarly productivity and nebulous, long-range goals of tenure or promotion, which alone so easily lead to overwork, exhaustion, and burnout. Any woman of color in academia who intends to excel and remain healthy and happy has to identify safe spaces for mentorship, collaboration, and peer support and resist the notion that needing help or feeling exhausted at times means that you're an imposter or cannot hack it in academia. You can hack it. You belong.

Jones builds on Williams's insights:

> One thing that's interesting and probably telling is that [women faculty of color] don't really use the language of burnout even if they are burned out. When you think of really high-achieving Black women, for instance, burnout is not a conversation that's had, because, well, of course you just keep going. Of course you do—why wouldn't you? You always have to achieve the next achievement. That's something a lot of my clients struggle with, needing to have the next achievement. And if they don't have the next achievement, then they think they're doing something wrong.
>
> Emotion also plays an important role here. In academia, we tend to reject emotions as frivolous or feminine. A Black woman can't have big emotions in public. So she might think, "I really have to be buttoned up and not admit that I need help with something. Never ask for help. Never advocate for myself in a way that's perceived as aggressive." And internalizing so much in and of itself becomes a major issue, just the feeling that there's really no one I can ask for help because they won't understand exactly what kind of help I need, especially when I'm the only Black person in the department.
>
> Women faculty of color have the extra weight of service and emotional labor, feeling that it is their job to support students of color and diversity initiatives. They might think, "No one else can do it. I am duty bound to do this. And if I don't, it's morally bad. This is my obligation to my community and to my students. My students need this." It's an unwinnable situation.

I've tried to respect voices such as these who do not, or are not ready to, discuss burnout at either the personal or the cultural levels, and I acknowledge the challenges associated with identities intersecting with higher ed.

Breaking Down Academic Identity

As I headed into burnout, I was what you might call an "unhappy achiever," and I sincerely doubt that I was the only one in higher ed. A term I first saw in a *Psychology Today* blog written by the psychotherapist Josh Dodes (2019), *unhappy achiever* refers to a high performer with many accomplishments who pursues each achievement with the possibly subconscious goal of external validation of their personal and professional worth. Unhappy achievers push themselves to attain everhigher goals, but it's never enough. According to Lance Dodes (2017), "They feel that they have to achieve *just to feel valuable or worthy*. Achievements aren't a joy; they're a necessity. . . . Stop achieving, and they stop being lovable. It's a terrible burden." He also notes that because high achievers rarely let anyone see them sweat, the people they care about might not realize that they are in trouble or suffering.

While not everyone in higher ed has an unhealthy relationship with achievement and satisfaction in their work, the different strands of literature on imposter syndrome, perfectionism, professional narcissism, and other-oriented achievement seem to link back to the same place. Higher ed as a culture and system places more value on external validation—peer review, promotion and tenure, grant funding, student evaluations, and so on—than on personal satisfaction or contentment for a job well done. We aren't taught to find satisfaction in our work for the work's sake; we are taught that external validation is what sustains us in our careers, according to Josh Dodes. As I fell deeper and deeper into burnout, my identity as a successful academic morphed into that of unhappy achiever and then into something much darker that was hard to overcome.

As I share in chapter 3, my professional identity was grounded in the "fact" that I had failed at my first (and only) industry job. When I left that job weeks before I would have been fired, I chose to return to grad school for a PhD because higher ed was the only place where my identity felt stable and had the potential to be fully actualized. Lieff and colleagues (2012, e208) draw from the work of John Paul Gee (2001), who they say described identity as encompassing "how individuals understand themselves, how they interpret experiences, how they present themselves and wish to be perceived by others and how they are recognized by the broader community." Identities are constructed over time, layered over familial, ethnic, and national contexts that shape who we are (Billot 2010, 711).

Studies have explored how academics create their professional identities. Broadly speaking, identities are never fixed, as they are socially constructed by every act, interaction, and shifting context. Billot (2010) argues that an "academic self" is constructed through a combination of one's idealized understanding of what an academic is and does as well as past and current interpretations of context (711–12). The academic identity is "intrinsically bound up with the values, beliefs and practices held in common with others of that affiliation," that is, the discipline, institution, or higher ed in general (712).

And academic identities in particular are fragile because every possible success in our careers is dependent on approval from others, never the satisfaction of a job well done when we publish an article in a top journal, get consistently high teaching evaluations, or get statistically significant results from a research study (Watts 1977). Knights and Clarke (2014) point out that "a person's social significance [and therefore identity] could easily be disturbed, disrupted, and reshaped by changes in social relations, particularly in the most important site of adult identity construction—the workplace" (338).

Thinking about burnout as a workplace phenomenon, academic identity hinges on the intersections between institution, discipline, and higher ed cultures, essentially the workplaces of academics. Add the competing intersections between what teaching, research, and service mean in this context, and identity becomes more complex as the borders blur. Knights and Clarke (2014) summarize Ford, Harding, and Learmonth (2010), Harley (2002), and Hearn (2008) to point out that academic culture, as our academic identities, are steeped in "competitiveness, intellectualism, achievement-orientation, hierarchy, and evaluativeness[, which may give rise to] all manner of high emotions, anxieties, defenses, denials, deceptions, and self-deceptions, rivalries, insecurities, threats, vulnerabilities, [and] intimacies" (338, quoting Hearn 2008, 190). It's hard not to see the conditions for burnout here.

Given that unstable foundation, my identity was always already tenuous. It was constructed on the beliefs that I could not succeed in industry, that higher ed was the only space where I belonged, and that I could only excel as an academic. I hung my entire professional identity on these beliefs and worked as hard as I could to prove them true. I clung to my sense of what it meant to be an academic and what my role was at and beyond my institution. And I fell into the traps of imposter syndrome and perfectionism.

Amy also struggled in a role that forced her to think about her academic identity differently and face its impact.

I've wanted to be a professor since I was a sophomore in high school. This is kind of strange for several reasons: one, because neither of my parents earned a college degree, and two, because no one ever told me what a professor was or did; it just seemed to be what fit with my ideal job at the time, the fact that I loved writing, and that I was good at school. Years later, as I was applying to get into a master's program, I was at a fork in the road—I still wanted to be a professor, but I felt I had seen a whole long list of "what not to do or be" as a professor in my undergrad years and was unsure of how to proceed. Understanding how to be a good educator won out, so I applied to a local master of education program. What I did not realize (since my undergrad degree was not in education) was that it was a major educational moment, the height of the No Child Left Behind and Highly Qualified Teacher movements. Thus, the master's experience was truly eye-opening. Surrounded by high-school teachers who were only in the classes because they had to be, I learned a lot about navigating classroom and administrative politics, how to creatively think about a course, and ways to be an advocate for students, but I also saw for the first time what true bitterness looked like in educators.

After graduating with my PhD (which also is not in education), I accepted a non-tenure-track teaching position—not necessarily my "ideal" job coming out of a big R1 flagship school. I was taught to be a researcher, and I love writing, but the teaching position has made it difficult to keep up with my desire to do scholarship and writing, especially since there are no benefits or requirements for me to do so.

And it becomes even more difficult to keep up because I tend to teach more than necessary, taking on as many overloads as possible. (I am only required to teach six courses per year; however, in the last eight years or so I have taught fifteen to nineteen classes each calendar year, often teaching five to six per quarter and almost never all having the same course prep.) I am not an adjunct, and I have a multiyear contract, so why do I do this? For several reasons: (a) to support living in a very expensive and ever-growing city; (b) to pay for student loans and credit-card debt from grad school; (c) to help out my once working-class but now retired parents;

and (*d*) to be able to buy things I need and/or want. Growing up working class and as a first-generation college student, I value living comfortably even if it means teaching triple my actual load and taking on extra side jobs on top of that. So yes, I have picked up extra jobs on top of all that teaching, which means that finding time to do scholarship and/or write is just incredibly difficult.

"You'll be a chain-smoking bitter [bitch] before you're 40" are words spoken to me several years ago by a person in authority, without the hopefulness that sometimes accompanies criticism. These words were said to me in a meeting at which I, armed with the ammunition of reasons why I deserved it, asked for a pay raise. This person and I had had a tumultuous relationship at best, so it was not surprising that the conversation was not positive. The words conveyed not concern but more of a threat about where I was headed, and they met with confusion on my part since I had been hoping for a raise so I *wouldn't* have to teach so much. Needless to say, I did not get the raise; thus, I continue to teach just as many classes.

But what makes it especially difficult is that now, almost four years after those words were spoken, I *am* bitter, no longer the once optimistic girl who just wanted to be a good educator. As the years march forward, and as I do inch closer to 40, the glittering hopefulness of my 20-something grows dimmer, swallowed up by mounds of debt, student papers, and teaching prep. And yet there's still a part of her in me harkening to break out and beyond the bitter B. I just don't know how.

Shaking Off the Imposter

The experienced coach and higher ed professional Katie Linder told me in a conversation about burnout and coaching that almost every academic client she's ever worked with has had some level of imposter syndrome that regularly impacted the way they thought about themselves and their work. As a social construct, identity hinges on constant renegotiation as a person participates in different aspects of a culture; as such, it is "interactive, fluid, and molded by situated work experiences that impact academics' understanding of their professional self and role" (Hutchins and Rainbolt 2017, 197; Jawitz 2009).

When you build a life around your mind and are surrounded by equal if not better minds, imposter syndrome is always lurking around the corner. Imposter syndrome, or imposter phenomenon, is the sense that one is inferior to those around one and that one will eventually be outed as not smart enough, innovative enough, or productive enough to belong in academia (Clance and Imes 1978; Hutchins and Rainbolt 2017; Knights and Clarke 2014).

In their implacable drive for achievement and expectation escalation, imposters often experience high levels of stress and burnout and are fed by "relentless pursuit of achievement, tempered by their inability to accept recognition when success is achieved, [which] often leads them to experience increased levels of stress and burnout, as well as declining job performance and overall satisfaction longitudinally" (Hutchins and Rainbolt 2017, 195, summarizing Whitman and Shanine 2012). And like burnout, the pressure to avoid being found out as incompetent, just lucky, or weak can lead to motivation and creative output but also deep self-doubt, pain, even despair (Alvesson 2009,198; Hutchins and Rainbolt 2017, 194).

Kristi Rudenga and Emily O. Gravett share their research into imposter phenomenon:

Impostor phenomenon (henceforth IP; colloquially known as "impostor syndrome") is rampant in higher education, particularly for certain social identities and at points of career transition. It can lead its subjects to believe, often despite extensive evidence to the contrary, that they do not deserve the success or position they have achieved. The main signs of IP, according to seminal research, are a belief that one has fooled others into overestimating one's abilities; an attribution of personal success to factors other than one's ability or intelligence, such as luck or an evaluator's misjudgment; and a fear of exposure as an impostor (Harvey and Katz 1985).

IP has been shown to negatively impact an individual's self-esteem, professional goal-directedness, locus of control, mood, and relationships with others (Brems et al. 1994). As Beth McMillan (2016) has written, "Many of the most respected academics in the world wake up every morning convinced that they are not worthy of their position, that they are faking it, and that they will soon be found out." Faculty members have been prolific in sharing their experiences of IP (see, e.g., Bahn 2014; Gravois 2007; Kasper 2013; Keenan 2016; and Rippeyoung 2012), and even those whose roles are dedicated to supporting faculty (e.g., faculty or educational developers) are not immune, as our research has shown (see Rudenga and Gravett 2019).

Our research suggests that there are several common consequences of IP. In a recent study (Rudenga and Gravett 2021), some survey respondents described the experience of IP as highly isolating; one wrote, for example, "I've had to use a lot of mental and emotional energy to 'squash' the IP so that I could perform in the given situation. It takes a lot of energy to 'hide' IP." Other respondents said that they feel compelled to "work extra hard and be twice as good" just to feel adequate at their job. They described "over-preparation" and "putting in many extra hours prepping . . . because [they] want to be perceived as knowledgeable." One subject reports, "I over achieve and over produce . . . because I feel like I am starting in a hole, I have to fill that hole before I can actually get work done." While many of these respondents presented hiding and over-work as viable coping strategies for dealing with IP, this response is troubling on both an individual and a structural level, as we have written elsewhere (Rudenga and Gravett 2021).

Unfortunately, for those feeling undeserving, fraudulent, and alone, the mere addition of more work is unlikely to result in a dissipation of IP . . . and can easily lead to burnout. Furthermore, the groups that may be most subject to IP, notably women and/or underrepresented minorities (Clance and Imes 1978; Cokley et al. 2017; Dancy and Brown 2011) have also historically felt isolated and alone at institutions while simultaneously being expected to take on extra (often undesirable and undervalued) work, for example, through teaching, advising, and service (see, e.g., O'Meara, Terosky, and Neumann 2008). Thus, the recommendation that these already overburdened individuals work harder in order to reduce or eradicate IP is highly problematic and closely tied to faculty burnout.

I'll come back to Rudenga and Gravett later in this section. In addition to what we know from the research about imposter syndrome, we can learn more about it and about how it might connect to and be addressed along with burnout by looking at it from different perspectives. On my podcast, *the agile academic*, the educator and faculty development professional Karen Costa shared her perspective that women in higher ed might experience imposter syndrome as internalized patriarchy (2021):

What if we reconsider imposter syndrome as internalized patriarchy? I hear a lot of women talking about imposter syndrome, and I don't love that phrase. I think it puts blame on the individual, like it's deficiency-based, and I just don't feel like it empowers women. Something that's been helpful to me is to reframe that and to say, "Oh, well, guess what, when every day of your life you've been told to be quiet and to not rock the boat and to follow these rules that have been set for women." And then you step outside of that, it's going to be excruciating. It's going to be really uncomfortable. It's going to create fear or terror or anxiety. I think renaming that from imposter syndrome to internalized patriarchy helps me to say, "Oh, okay, then I'm just going to have to move through this."

The psychologist and coach Kristina Hallett (2020) offers another perspective, that imposter syndrome is an evolutionary holdover from our need to be a member of the tribe for our own safety:

> Imposter syndrome, that feeling that you just don't belong, is an ongoing issue in nearly 70% of the population across gender, race, profession, and age, and is far from being a simple sign of self-doubt or insecurity. Imposter syndrome is significantly associated with burnout and frequently results in perfectionism and procrastination. And it's a barrier to productivity regardless of the setting. Neurological research findings pointed to a widespread effect from imposter syndrome of greater unhappiness, greater tension and anxiety, decreased productivity from burnout and a decrease in healthy risks, such as speaking up in a meeting or going for a promotion. That's a lot of impact related to a few thoughts....
>
> And we tend to view the idea of failure or imperfection as highly stressful and dangerous. Since we know that imposter syndrome is almost universally experienced, we can consider that imposter syndrome is more like a reflexive brain response than an accurate expression of

abilities. From an evolutionary perspective, we needed to be part of the tribe. So, the fear of getting ostracized, it was pretty dangerous. But we can recognize that imposter syndrome is a normal reaction. It's our brain's way of naturally responding. It's not a sign that you don't belong. It's a sign that you're human.

Based on their research, Holly Hutchins and Hilary Rainbolt (2017) argue that we must normalize having conversations about mental health and imposter phenomenon because, as with burnout, there is a shame attached to being "found out" as weak or vulnerable (209). Rudenga and Gravett agree, as we return to their work:

> A more productive strategy—and one that showed up frequently in the descriptions of research subjects who reported IP as a memory of something they dealt with previously—is to connect with others around the experience. One subject reported that "having open conversations about IP has brought a unity and closeness with colleagues"; others echoed the sentiment that vulnerability and openness with trusted colleagues was a key to coping with or overcoming IP.
>
> It is worth noting the key step here: positive consequences and progress in mitigating IP only emerge after "revealing" or "having open conversations about" IP. This stands in stark contrast to the responses above, which described IP as highly isolating, with respondents feeling they had to "hide" or "squash" their IP. While there may be risks involved in revealing impostor feelings, depending on one's positionality and particular context, such vulnerability seems to make the difference between IP being a disconnecting experience and a connecting one, an ongoing battle and a memory. For those suffering from burnout as a result of IP, we suggest seeking

out trustworthy, empathetic colleagues and mentors, whether from within your institution or elsewhere, to share your feelings and to begin to build community. A happy benefit is that vulnerability often begets vulnerability, as Brown's research has shown (2017), and so by sharing your own experiences of IP, you may help others to open up and find connection and community too.

Additional strategies for coping with and mitigating IP without the battle contributing to burnout include reviewing your experience and accomplishments to remind yourself that you have, in fact, earned your position; accepting that some tasks will not be done perfectly (and embracing a growth mindset); focusing on your strengths; and getting comfortable with improvising (Kaplan 2009).

When a faculty member experiences burnout from overwork, due not only to an artificially diminished perception of their own abilities and achievements, but also to a perception that they are the only person who feels and must struggle this way, then one important antidote would be to identify this experience as IP, become aware that they are not alone, connect with colleagues over IP in a meaningful way, and consider more sustainable coping strategies.

As I discuss later in the book, self-compassion and human connection are paths through burnout. But other tendencies, like imposter syndrome and perfectionism, can cloud that path. If I am (or was) an unhappy achiever, I'm also a perfectionist, and during my burnout I worked hard and successfully to hide what I was going through, denying myself the opportunity for both compassion (chapter 4) and connection (chapter 5). Perfectionism is another underlying identity feature that can both manifest or be revealed in burnout.

Perfecting Your Academic Identity

I have always set (often unrealistically) high standards for myself, which eventually spilled over into my expectations of colleagues and even my students. Those standards didn't just include my work; I wanted everyone around me, including family, to think I had it all together and was doing brilliantly at life and career. This showed up in weird ways, such as hiring a painter at the very last minute to paint half of my home's downstairs to impress my parents (they couldn't have cared less as long as I was happy) or panic-buying new conference wardrobes so that everyone around me knew I was living my best life, even when I was miserable on the inside. It manifested in my professional anxiety, cleverly disguised as competitive spirit, that I would be overlooked for leadership opportunities or my work would be scooped at any minute, so I had to be always serving, writing, publishing, excelling, and producing to be my ideal academic self. But ideals are hard to live up to.

T. Elon Dancy II and Jean-Marie Gaetane (2014) define perfectionism as the "belief that work or output that is anything less than perfect is unacceptable," and they include among the aspects of perfectionism depending on external measure of success, holding unrealistic standards, experiencing negative emotions such as anxiety and guilt related to work, and being unable to process failures as anything other than personal failing (361). Elements of narcissism and Type A personality may be present as well (Jamal and Baba 2001; Westerman et al. 2016). Nagoski and Nagoski (2019) contend that "a lot of us spend our lives pushing ourselves to work harder, do more, be better; feeling failure when we fall short of someone's expectation; and chastising ourselves for 'being arrogant' if we celebrate success or 'settling' if we accept something short of perfection" (196).

Perfectionism for me was likely a combination of nature and nurture; perfectionism was my strategy for both career success and coping with letdowns and rejection. When perfectionism as a coping strategy against stress reaches toxic levels, burnout results (Nagoski and Nagoski 2019, 194–95). In Hutchins and Rainbolt's 2017 study, faculty experiencing imposter syndrome and toxic perfectionism dealt with imposter events "in harmful ways through negative self-talk, inaccurate attributions concerning success and failure, and [further] perfectionistic work tendencies" (207). They note that those with a bent to perfectionism spent a great deal of energy working to hide any trace of "weakness" or inadequacy, which led to higher instances of burnout (208).

Brené Brown's (2012, 2017) definition of narcissism might also be a definition of perfectionism: "When I look at narcissism through the lens of vulnerability, I see the shame-based fear of being ordinary. I see fear of never feeling extraordinary enough to be noticed, to be lovable, to belong, or to cultivate a sense of purpose" (Brown 2012, 22). Being ordinary or unnoticed, as I shared earlier, was a deep-seated fear that drove me to judge myself and those around me by accomplishments. Similarly, Kelly J. Baker (2017) interrogated this drive as follows: "[My] melodramatic focus on accomplishments was not ever about my life, but the career that I thought I wanted. It was a to-do list that a younger version of me created. My plan equated life with career and career with success. A career is not a life. What an impoverished vision of success dependent on external validation and a weird obsession with success as our only option. Accomplishments are an awful way to measure the value of a life" (77).

A career is not a life. That was one of the hardest lessons I had to learn when dealing with my burnout and perfectionism. It was a challenging lesson for Lara as well:

When I was hired in 2000, my desire to please and to be seen as the perfect colleagues and "team player" made me susceptible to the opaque request for "help" with an administrative position in addition to a three-course teaching load. I had good training for this particular job, which was directing a federally funded National Writing Project (NWP) site. I had been through an NWP summer institute, and I had had a rare course in Writing Program Administration. Yet beneath all of this was a powerful sense that eventually someone would find out how uncertain and unconfident I still was.

So, when I was asked if I would "help out" with the Writing Project, I said yes, taking some comfort that I would be assisting in something I was familiar with. However, I didn't understand that this job consumed summer and winter breaks because it required raising matching funds, writing multiple reports, and leading a summer institute. I also didn't understand that instead of *assisting* the current director, I was meant to *replace* her. She felt like the department didn't value her hard work because she had *only* earned a master's degree, and here they were hiring me, with a newly minted PhD, to take credit for her work. This pressure quickly led to *her* emotional breakdown, which manifested as a drunken tirade at myself and some teachers during a conference, my colleague accusing us of sabotage. This was my first professional year. I began to drink a lot myself.

When it came time for tenure, I learned that the work of the directorship had caused my then department head to be denied promotion and tenure when he had directed the NWP back when he was a new professor. He hadn't met the publication requirements because he had devoted his time to writing NWP grant proposals and reports. When this same situation happened to me, he shrugged. "Oh well," he said. "Write an appeal to the dean," he said.

I became paralyzed by anxiety, unable on many mornings to get out of bed. I had lots of hangovers. I called in sick a lot.

Once, when my then-boyfriend was doing some carpentry for a colleague, I called all the local hospitals and the police station looking for him because my colleague had said he hadn't returned to her house from lunch. I got completely swept up in the friend's paranoia; she was also battling the tenure process. In reality, he had been eating a sandwich in his truck after a run to the hardware store. When I told him this story in tears that afternoon, he told me very calmly that if I didn't get a grip, he would leave.

So I got a grip. I got a therapist and some anti-anxiety meds and finally got some clarity about the root of my anxiety. The meds helped me calm down enough to face my anxiety, explore it, and change my relationship to it. I married the boyfriend, weaned slowly off the meds, began taking care of my inner life. I was able to quit blood pressure medicine and smoking and to get more control over the drinking. Part of the difference is that I feel joy and gratitude at my core, even when infuriating or devastating events arise.

Things aren't perfect, but I am much more comfortable with that imperfection; in fact, I see the great damage of perfectionism: it fed my imposter syndrome for years. As Ann Lamott writes [in *Bird by Bird* (1995)], "Perfectionism means that you try desperately not to leave so much mess to clean up.... Clutter is wonderfully fertile ground—you can still discover new treasures under all those piles, clean things up, edit things out, fix things, get a grip." ... With steady practice, I have become ok with ambiguity and uncertainty, because I know that those will pass, just like clouds and thoughts and feelings, in rhythm with our breathing, the tides, the turning earth.

What Lara and I experienced led to what David Machell (1988) labeled "professional melancholia." As summarized by Carolyn Oxenford and Sally Kublenschmidt (2011), professional melancholia is a precursor to burnout:

> This progressive deterioration of self-esteem and emotional health begins when young professors with unrealistic expectations of perfection and approval discover that they are no longer star students. Professional competition and inevitable rejections lead to increasing levels of hurt, resentment, and frustration. The faculty member begins to build a self-protective wall that leads to further loss of motivation, decreased scholarly interest, and lowered self-esteem. At its most extreme, professional melancholia can result in contempt for students and colleagues, deep alienation, elitism, and arrogance. (188)

For many women in higher ed, perfectionism can be rooted in academic identity perhaps as both a feature of our natural personalities and a nurtured characteristic of how one shows up for this work, work that is judged by others at every turn and in which we were never trained to find satisfaction or contentedness. When perfectionism, similarly to imposter syndrome, takes over, burnout is a logical extension of that mind-set.

Conclusion

In one of their foundational studies in the field, Maslach, Schaufeli, and Leiter (2001) argue that "burnout is higher among individuals who have an external locus of control, possess other-oriented empathy, and are more emotional than cognitive" (p. 410). For many of the women I interviewed these traits were part of their academic identity; they certainly were part of mine. My RPR persona juggled these traits by locking

ARTICULATING PIECES OF ACADEMIC IDENTITY

Much of our identity is formed over time on the basis of stories we tell ourselves about our life and experience. The stories we tell ourselves can feed coping strategies like perfectionism, as well as unfortunately common issues like imposter syndrome.

We all tell ourselves stories that become calcified over time, to the point that we don't question them anymore. To surface some of those beliefs, consider these fill-in-the-blanks:

- My greatest weakness as a professional is *W*. I know this is a weakness I have because *X*. This weakness causes me *Y* problems. If I could "fix" this weakness, I might be able to *Z*.
- When I experience imposter syndrome, I am usually in [*what situation? with whom?*]. This situation kicks off my self-doubt because [*reasons*]. This is a problem for me in my professional or even personal life because [*reasons*]. I just wish I could [*what?*].
- Being perceived as doing perfect work is important to me because [*reasons*]. When I don't live up to perfection, I worry that it means [*what?*]. When I am perceived as perfect, I feel [*how?*], which is good because [*reasons*] but also negative because [*reasons*].

Now let's flip those scripts:

- My greatest strength as a professional is *X*. I first developed this strength by *Y*, and this strength serves me well because *Z*.
- I know that I am adept at [*something*], and this benefits my professional self because [*reasons*]. I can use this strength to [*do what?*], and that's important to me because [*reasons*].
- When I experience imposter syndrome, I am usually in [*what situation? with whom?*]. When I think about why imposter feelings are arising, I remind myself [*what?*] so that I can [*do what?*].
- Doing meaningful work is important to me because [*reasons*]. I don't live or work to be perfect but instead want [*what?*]. I know I have achieved meaningful work when I [*what?*], and this is important to me because it reminds me [*what?*].

What insights did you reveal when you flipped the script?

down my emotions almost completely, drastically limiting the level of compassion I had for students and peers, and pretending I wasn't living for the next achievement and recognition. RPR became so detached that I lost my sense of purpose for doing the work I had once loved and the students I had once championed, found it nearly impossible to show compassion, withdrew from the connections with students and peers that I had once enjoyed, and found myself focusing on work all the time (see Schubert-Irastorza and Fabry 2014).

Multiple studies show that women faculty who are burning out are most prone to exhaustion, while male faculty are more likely to depersonalize as a coping strategy for unrelenting workplace stress (see, e.g., Lackritz 2004; and Schubert-Irastorza and Fabry 2014). But there remains that need to protect ourselves and our academic identities. Oxenford and Kublenschmidt (2011) note that faculty become adept at concealing problems from others and even from themselves, which means that they may not seek help or be seen fully by others (189). As in other chronic stress and emotional health situations, acknowledging that something is wrong and the ways it is impacting life and work is the crucial first step to dealing with burnout and some of the less than healthy aspects of our academic identities.

In the chapters that follow, I introduce four lenses through which to look at and, one hopes, mitigate burnout as a consequence of higher ed's sometimes toxic culture and the academic identities women build in that culture. By exploring purpose, compassion, connection, and balance, we can address burnout in ourselves and our peers to start making changes at the individual level that can then spiral outward to impact the entire culture.

These Bootstraps Are Choking Me:
The Working-Class Burnout of a
First-Gen College Professor

VALERIE MURRENUS PILMAIER

I'd imagine that every single teacher in America has suffered from or is currently suffering from burnout. In my case, in addition to regular teaching burnout, I also have the longitudinal burnout of being a female former first-generation college student now tenured in academia. Translation: for years, I constantly second-guessed myself, felt the need to prove myself, did not feel content with anything of merit that I had achieved, often felt like a failure, and had difficulty saying no when asked to do something. You are probably thinking, "Oh, imposter syndrome." Sure, that is part of it, but it is so much more than that. My sense of exhaustion stems from a lifetime of negotiating the slipperiness that comes from shape-shifting class identities in order to survive in higher education.

In America, we like to think that class affects nothing, when it actually affects everything. Social class informs the way we understand and navigate the world. While it is everyone's dream in America to be upwardly mobile, thus "bettering" themselves with each successive generation, very few people discuss the growing pains that are born from that transition. I am the crossroads between my parents' working-class ethos and my children's middle-class ease. I am a battleground constantly at war.

When I started college, it felt like walking into the Upside Down. There were classes, which was familiar, but the assignment expectations, time management requirements, and social performances were overwhelming. I chose not to attend the college close to home with all of my friends because I wanted to branch out, but that meant that I had no one to turn to when I had questions. My parents were clueless and had little sympathy for my complaints after having worked ten-hour days to finance my time at school. I felt I had to account for every cent they had invested in me. I thought everyone understood how college worked except for me. I was too proud to ask for help even if I knew who to ask because I didn't want to look like I didn't belong. My parents were depending on me. I had to kill at this.

Just as I had done as a latchkey kid with too much time on my hands, I escaped into books. While other kids my age were out partying, I was in the stacks of the library picking out the books that would be "my date" for that weekend. I hated the party atmosphere and had no idea it was even possible to transfer to a different college. My parents brought me up on "bootstrap theory," so I felt that if I worked hard enough, my brain would save me. If I were smart enough, and knew all of the answers, if I researched enough and wrote great papers, I would master college. I eventually got the hang of it, but that was in spite of the terrible advisers who had no time for me. It was so much easier if I read the catalog and figured it out myself. I had to figure it out myself because only those who didn't belong had to ask for help, and I belonged, right? I was not sorry to leave upon graduation.

In grad school I found a home. While many students came from families with intergenerational college-educated backgrounds, there were also some who were just like me. We sought one another out and bonded, mocking what was incomprehensible and luxuriating in the realization that we were being trained for white-collar jobs. We were The American Dream.

While a star in my previous English department, I was a state school kid, and almost everyone else came from private schools, so I worried that my training was subpar by comparison. Again, relying on my working-class ethos, I dug in and did more research, perfected the art of essay writing for seminar classes, and threw myself into teaching. With each new assignment, I fell into crippling self-doubt. I flew through my MA and PhD coursework and then hit a wall at ABD: my dissertation felt like a bully, humiliating me at every turn.

Who was I kidding? Me a professor? The future became a possibility once I passed my exams. How could I pretend that I deserved *Doctor* before my name? How dare I be so pretentious? My fear of status and writing that dissertation crippled me for years. Well, that and having to cobble together four different adjuncting gigs to pay the bills. Writing, which had once been my greatest joy, now made me sick. No one gave me advice, but nor did I ask for any, and my dissertation adviser repeated, "I'm not worried about you." Yet, I was worried about me; I had to build a foundation without having any of the tools or the confidence to do it. I finally finished my dissertation, but every word was agony.

Almost immediately, I got a job on the tenure track and felt the need to prove that I deserved to be there. Self-doubt pushed me to exhaustion: I bent over backwards to be the best colleague, the most dedicated professor, and a productive scholar while balancing being a wife and mother. I developed insomnia, extreme anxiety, and blinding headaches. Secretly, I often hit the panic button. I did not know how to ask for help. I did not realize that I could or should ask for help.

After tenure, I realized that my own sense of class inferiority had created this demon: the only person who had felt that I didn't belong in any of those earlier scenarios was me. I had created an impossible standard to achieve because I felt that I needed to "work harder" when no one else expected that of me. I now delegate and ask for help, have learned to value my own time and say no when I can't/don't want to do something. There will always be a demon on my shoulder saying, "You aren't working enough," but I now say, "Yes, I am."

CHAPTER 3

Purpose

A goal is not a life—but it may be what gives shape
and direction to the way we live each day.
—Emily Nagoski and Amelia Nagoski

Here's a confession: I only started my PhD program because I (almost) got fired from the real world.

In the spring of 2002, I asked my boss, the owner of a boutique marketing-communications firm in Silicon Valley, if we could have a meeting at the end of the day. For the three weeks prior, I had been on probation, and Bob had given me a long list of things I had to do or prove to keep my job, my first grown-up job as a marketing agency writer. The day he expressed his dissatisfaction with my work and gave me the ultimatum, I somehow made it home to the house I shared with two other women and our landlord, who used our dining room as the hub of her real estate business. I fell catatonic onto my bed as soon as I shut the door to my room, not moving from the same spot until the next morning. And he'd given me the news on a Friday, so I had to sit with it all weekend. Once I could rouse myself, I tried to think of a plan to be more successful and to become the expert writer I thought I already was. But it quickly became clear that nothing would be good enough for him.

Back in Bob's office before the end of my probation period, I did what any reasonable overachiever whose worth depended on her intelligence and success would do: I quit. I quit before he could fire me because his list was totally unrealistic, expecting me to write as if I were a ten-year veteran, and I knew I'd never be able to meet his unrealistic demands. My clients at the firm were happy with my work, but it was never good enough for Bob, never enough "valued added" for his taste. So, I gave my two weeks' notice and fed him a line that I wanted to move back east and go for my PhD.

I came to find out, after I had some distance, that Bob fired or pushed out all of his writers before eighteen months so he didn't have to pay into COBRA insurance. But at the time, I was devastated. I had *failed*. I'd never failed before and wasn't even sure how I'd managed to fail this time. The story I began to tell myself of that failure was that I wasn't cut out for nonacademic work; hence the lie about going to grad school rather than just saying I quit because he was a jerk. I did think I would be safe in higher ed. I knew how to succeed there, right?

So I moved back into my parents' house in Pittsburgh, totally humiliated, and looked for temporary work. I halfheartedly emailed some graduate programs to ask for information about applying for the 2003–4 cohort since the deadlines for starting in the fall had long passed. Lo and behold, I received an email that there was still room in the 2002–3 cohort in my top program choice, and within two weeks I was accepted into the program and moving to Iowa, where, coincidentally, my California boyfriend was from and where he had just moved after getting laid off. See, it was a sign that academia was where I was supposed to be.

This professional "failure" colored the rest of my adult life and work. Through my teaching and research during my five years of graduate school and later in my tenure-track role, I regained a sense of self, but that self was firmly wrapped up in the quest for success and relevance, possibly so as not to have to go back into industry, where failure was inevitable. I was empowered and empowering, the knowledgeable expert, holder of high standards, designer of transformational learning opportunities for my beloved students. I volunteered for service roles and workshops, anything to raise my profile and prove I belonged. I published. Co-curricularly, I even advised the campus chapter of my sorority, often on campus on weekends for meetings and chaperoning formals. (Yes, chaperoning formals is as awful as it sounds.)

Looking back, I see that teaching and advising soothed my fear of being unsuccessful or unimportant or a failure because I was *needed* in those roles. But being needed or relevant or productive is not a purpose for a career or a life. It was a response to an unspeakable fear that I was not enough for higher ed, the only place I thought I belonged. Life became much more about proving to people that I belonged in higher ed than about supporting students, putting out research that helped my peers teach well, or serving my discipline and institution. But that wears on you over time, depletes energy, fatigues the reserves of compassion that were once so deep. So the walls start going up, little by little, the exhaustion, cynicism, martyring. And the burnout creeps in slowly, then takes over in a flash when you can no longer see your purpose clearly or see your work as meaningful.

But there was resilience in purpose, even in the breakdown of these fears and values.

Reflection Opportunity

- What is your current relationship with your purpose?
- What's the most meaningful reason that you do your work?
- Who do you need to be to pursue your purpose?
- How will you know when you are pursuing your true purpose?
- If you were pursuing your true purpose, what would the ideal outcome be?

What Is Fulfilling Work in Higher Ed?

When I ask faculty members what their purpose is or what fulfills them, I usually get a range of answers. On the most positive and idealistic end, I hear things like "I'm shaping problem-solvers/citizens/artists of tomorrow" and "My research with zebrafish may lead to a significant finding in the treatment of cancer." But at the other end of the spectrum, I hear something quite different: "I need to make it through this week, and then the next, and then the next" and "If I can just survive this semester, I'll be OK." How do we get from the peak of Maslow's hierarchy of needs all the way down to the base of his triangle, the way I certainly did?

Many of us come to higher education with a level of idealism and determination to make a difference through some combination of teaching, research, and service to the community. Maybe an undergraduate course

---

DEFINING YOUR PURPOSE, YOUR MISSION

Before diving into the chapter, take a moment to create a few possible purpose statements that reflect what you care about now—not what higher ed cares about but what you as a person and a professional care about. Keep your statement in mind while exploring the chapter.

---

sparked a passion in you or a mentor recognized your potential as an academic. Maybe you had something to prove to someone, or to yourself. Or maybe like me, you felt most comfortable—the most "you"—in a university setting. You hope you find, to quote Alex Soojung-Kim Pang, "the work that gives your life meaning; the work that lets you be yourself and helps you become a better self; the work that is an unparalleled pleasure when it goes well and is worth fighting for when it goes poorly; the work you are willing to organize your life around. *I think we all have this work, and the quality of our lives is determined by how well we are able to do it*" (17–18, emphasis added). Pang's last statement gives me pause; it's especially relevant to higher education. What purpose drives us? What values ground us? How much of ourselves do we give to the work of higher ed? What is fulfilling and meaningful in this work—not ideally, but actually?

Without diving into the deep well of philosophy from Aristotle to Monty Python, and in the interest of brevity, I'll define my terms in the following way: *Values* are the firm beliefs and moral guides that inform everything we do. A *purpose* is what inspires us to do the work, a driving question, commitment, goal, contribution, or legacy that one pursues to make a difference in some way. *Meaning* is the value we derive from that pursuit. And *fulfillment* is the satisfaction of achieving one's potential and contentment. (Educational developers, see appendix 1 for an activity to help the faculty you work with define their legacy.) My thinking is shaped by Aristotle's value ethics in the sense that our highest purpose and motivation, intrinsic and extrinsic, should be to create our best selves.

Finding and fulfilling a purpose is an active journey as we work, thrive, and overcome to do so. It is not a static state, nor is it created for us externally.* In their book about women and burnout, Nagoski and

* Unless we give someone or something the power to make meaning for us.

Nagoski (2019) describe a sense of meaning and purpose as crucial to overcoming burnout when purpose is defined as "the nourishing experience of feeling like we're connected to something larger than ourselves. It helps us thrive when things are going well, and it helps us cope when things go wrong" (58). And it is this pursuit of a meaningful purpose guided by our values that can help us avoid or at least mitigate burnout.

Reflection Opportunity

- What would it look like to successfully fulfill your purpose?
- What motivates you most to fulfill your purpose, in general and in higher ed?
- What stories do you tell yourself about (pursuing) your purpose? What stories might you tell instead?

How Do Values Impact Our Purpose?

Before we explore purpose as a path to mitigate burnout, let's first consider and articulate values, an activity many of us might spend little, if any, time on. I think about values a lot since my burnout experience. I've been rethinking and rearticulating those values almost methodically in different ways, but it's hard work when you do it intentionally. Many of my values were formed long before graduate school competition or the pressure of the first tenure-track job. They were formed in elementary school, where I, like many "smart kids," was trained to see my value in the things faculty now lament our students overemphasize: grades, leadership, number of extracurriculars, and other activities, like service, that round out a successful college application (Hallett 2018, 15).

During my burnout, I was often asked in therapy or in wellness groups to complete a value-identifying exercise, which frustrated me no end because they made me confront the fact that my values were associated with productivity, success, excellence, achievement, being the best, and so on. (If you'd like to take a similar assessment, simply do an internet search for "values activity.") As much as I wanted to be able to say that things like integrity, happiness, and community were my core values, that would have been a stretch, even a lie. I associated so much of what I'd now identify as shame with being so externally motivated that I publicly mocked the exercise so as not to look deeply within myself and examine where those achievement-oriented values were really coming from. But I wouldn't be surprised to find that other academics feel the same way. It's trained into us, even if it wasn't part of our natural disposition beforehand.

On one hand, higher ed as a culture espouses the values of lifelong learning, discovery, contribution to a better world, and striving for excellence, all wrapped up in a view of the academy as a calling to change the world through research and teaching. I love these values as ideals. In a sense, I gave myself completely over to them, to the cultural imperative that the vaunted halls of higher education only call a few and that fewer still can belong successfully. For me, and for many faculty members with whom I've spoken, it was an overcommitment to the idea of being "called" that opened the door for our work to be all-encompassing, which sets us up for burnout.

When one has a calling instead of a job in higher ed, no matter how great the job is, it's much easier to slowly give more and more of yourself as you buy into the competitive achievement orientation of the academy and the culture, which will continue to pull more from you in service of the calling. Without a check-and-balance system, success becomes bound up in higher ed's other values: productivity, achievement, (over)work, and your ability to keep up with the expectation escalation and ladder climbing to the holy grail of tenure-track positions inherent in the academic career trajectory, as discussed in the chapter on culture.

I interviewed Katie Linder, a coach who works with academics:

> Some people come to higher ed because they have a deep value of personal and professional growth or lifelong learning, and what they're finding in higher ed is not aligned with that. For many people, higher ed is a great fit for their personal values. But in graduate school, you also experience the breakdown of your own personal sense of what you are supposed to be doing. You need to get constant approval from your peers, from your blind reviewers, from your adviser, or from your department chair and whatever board to get promotion and tenure. There's always someone else who's deciding your value. So, what does that do for your own decision making?

Linder's summary reminds me that there is great irony in my choosing academia after I considered my time in industry such a failure. Success in academia requires constant approval seeking, externalized motivations, and rejection, with so many decisions completely out of your hands, including article acceptances, book contracts, promotion and tenure, even landing a full-time position. So the move certainly wasn't into a culture with less stress, but it was a stress I understood.

When we depend on external validation, we see competition at every corner: "We only look at those ahead of us—and of course, there is no shortage of more productive, better cited and more well-known scholars than ourselves" (Bothello and Roulet 2019, 857). I deeply internalized competition and productivity as core values before burnout, partially because in the US education system we are trained to judge ourselves on "doing well rather than living well" (Hallett 2018, 15) and to "judge our days based on how efficient they are, not how fulfilling" (Headlee 2020, xii). As Brené Brown (2017) says of her own perfectionism, "I got sucked into proving I could, rather than stepping back and asking if I should—or if I even really wanted to" (194).

As I came out of burnout, I started to realize I could grow into other values and reshape my purpose in different ways. Nagoski and Nagoski contend that "our culture treats you as if 'being productive' is the most important measure of your worth, as if you are a consumable good. . . . You are not here to be 'productive.' You are here to be you, to engage with your Something Larger, to move through the world with confidence and joy" (184). If I could define excellence and success for myself, instead of looking for outside validation, I could finally revisit my purpose and how I make meaning of my life and work with a greater sense of who I am and who I wanted to be after burnout.

Katherine Segal offers a guided pathway for approaching burnout as an opportunity to reflect and recapture your purpose.

> As a coach and therapist, I have worked with hundreds of clients with the goal of implementing plans to change their behavior. I have found it essential to address resistance and motivation before implementing new behaviors as well as throughout the change process. With that in mind, I asked my study participants to describe their process of healing from burnout. Most described the experience of burnout as traumatic, and their motivation for behavioral change resembled post-traumatic growth. Further, they described burnout as a catalyst for reflecting critically on their lives, particularly assessing the time and energy taken up by their careers.
>
> Post-traumatic growth "refers to positive psychological change experienced as a result of the struggle with highly challenging life circumstances" (Tedeschi and Calhoun 2004, 1). In reflecting on this source of motivation, the participants described a strong desire to

engage in behaviors that would help them overcome burnout. Several participants attributed their growth to viewing burnout as an opportunity to transform their lives.

Another aspect of post-traumatic growth for the participants was devising a plan to create a sustainable career, which included the following steps:

1. *Begin by reflecting on your motivations for becoming an educator.* Maybe you have a strong passion for educating the next generation. Maybe you want to be the kind of educator who inspired you. Maybe you want to be the kind of educator you wish you had had throughout your years of schooling. Or, maybe being a professor is the only way to make a living in your field of study. Whatever your reason, write it down. Read it aloud. Revise. Continue reading it aloud and revising until you feel it fully captures your reasons for pursuing and entering the role of professor.

2. *Shift to thinking about why you want to remain an educator.* As before, whatever the rationale, write it down without judgment, read it aloud, and revise. Continue until your stated reasons for continuing in this profession (not this particular job) are clear and deeply resonate with you.

3. *Picture your future life.* Answer the following questions to add detail to your vision: If I were to wake up in my ideal life, what would I see, feel, or experience? As I move through my ideal day, where am I, what am I doing, and who am I with? How does my career fit into my ideal life? Consider these subquestions:
   a. What do I want to achieve throughout my career?
   b. How do I know I am being successful in my career?
   c. How much time do I spend on work responsibilities?
   d. How do I feel while engaging in work responsibilities?

As you form this vision in your mind, try to move through the scene from a first-person perspective rather than a third-person perspective. Notice how you feel emotionally and physically as you sit with this vision. As before, write this all down, read it aloud, and revise as needed. You aren't looking for the most polished piece of literature, but for for the answers that feel true to you. Completing this activity might be difficult at first for those who have spent a long time in the narrative of what we *should* want compared with what we *do* want. But just allow your experience of burnout to serve as the motivation for transforming your life.

A Note on Meaningfulness in Career Choices

Aligning our values with our purpose can be a source of deep meaning. When that alignment is off or others exert their values and purpose on you, it can be a source of burnout. Alaya Malach Pines (1993) and Bert Loonstra, Andre Brouwres, and Welko Tomic (2009) agree that when we do not feel as though our lives and work are meaningful, we open the door wide for burnout to enter. The existential crisis that can arise from such a misalignment is born in part from "cultural messaging everywhere that says an ordinary life is a meaningless life" (Brown 2012, 23), that the only good career in academia is one of constant striving for more and better, whether measured in teaching evaluations or grant money awarded, the number of committees led, or articles and books published with prestigious outlets.

Mai experienced this disconnect in conversations with administration about women and full professorships at her institution:

At one point I was having this intense conversation with some of our faculty who know our campus has some old sexist structures that we're trying to tear down. The choice to become tenured and associate and to stop there to build your career out in other ways has become frowned upon in ways that disadvantage women faculty members.

There have been conversations about careers and about how staying at the associate level is not enough. Administration wants programming to persuade more of our women to go for full, but I'd like to help women figure out if that's what they want to do. So I suggested a broader approach, examining the decision to go up for full professor more holistically. What have others done? What were their choices? What have they found fulfilling about those choices?

And I opened up a can of worms. It was as if there were nothing besides full professorship. Are you telling me that if I stay here another twenty years and accomplish all these goals that you've all told me are wonderful, if I can't say I'm a full professor when I retire, I'm not worthwhile, or I didn't have a good career? That's not a message we should be sending about what constitutes a meaningful career or one I'm willing to perpetuate. My goal is to help our women faculty create fulfilling careers aligned with their purpose and values, whether that includes going up for full professor or not.

Working with purpose and a sense of your true values provides guidance.

Reflection Opportunity

- If your biggest roadblock to following your purpose were removed, what would you do?
- At the end of your career, what will you be most proud of? What are steps you can take now to achieve that?

How Can We (Re)Find and (Re)Commit to Our Purpose?

In my discussion with Katie Linder about values and purpose, she shared some of what she sees in the academic women who come to her for coaching, especially mid- and later-career women faculty: "Many clients come into the coaching relationship confused about how they have found themselves here in their career, with it not feeling meaningful to them. They are feeling overwhelmed or apathetic about where things are going. Nothing feels exciting anymore. They start to kind of ask themselves, 'Is this it? Is this everything?' They've gotten to that point where they admit that they are no longer feeling fulfilled and start to question whether they felt fulfilled all along."

I certainly found this to be true several years after earning promotion and tenure, and that questioning of purpose was a contributor to my burnout and my burnout recovery. Who was I when I wasn't "doing" higher ed or striving to do and be more? What was the point of what I was doing in my research and service, even in my teaching? As the exhaustion and cynicism took over, I began to disengage—a key sign of burnout.

Much of the literature on burnout shows that an erosion of engagement with the job due to the chronic stress and struggle associated with work is a hallmark of the third element of burnout (Harrison 1999; Lackritz 2004; Maslach and Leiter 2015; Maslach, Schaufeli, and Leiter 2001). Maslach and Leiter note that fulfilling, meaningful engagement with one's work is diametrically opposed to the three elements of burnout: exhaustion, cynicism, and lack of feelings of efficacy. Characterized as "high levels of positive energy, determination, and dedication to getting the job done," engagement, then, is not just a mark of burnout resilience but also potentially a means of warding off burnout (Schubert-Irastorza and Fabry 2014, 42). In earlier work, Schaufeli and Bakker (2001, 2004) synthesized multiple studies to define work engagement as a "positive, fulfilling, work-related state of mind that is characterized by vigor, dedication, and absorption" (Schaufeli and Bakker 2004, 295).

So what have the women faculty and coaches I've spoken with found to be most engaging and fulfilling? Students, a focus on social justice, and work outside the academy.

Working with Students

One purpose that women faculty and coaches articulate over and over was working with students. Studies showed that while research often led to negative and anxiety-laden feelings, teaching was more often described as energizing, meaningful, enjoyable, and important. I always wanted to be a teacher more than a researcher, and I ultimately built my entire tenure case on the scholarship of teaching and learning (SoTL) because working with students, watching them grow as writers and future professionals, was significant and fulfilling. I loved being in the trenches with them when we did service-learning projects and client-based work. I got excited when I taught about the history of rhetoric or publishing, persuasive strategies to shape an effective grant narrative, or ways that project management is a rhetorical and a professional skill. I relished being able to share knowledge, help students shape good questions, and mentor students from different disciplines. I loved it all.*

But as I'll talk about in the chapter on connection, losing that joy and pulling away from students was one of the early signs of my burnout.

---

* Except the grading. I loved offering extensive feedback but hated assigning letters or numbers as if objectivity were really possible.

Eventually all three burnout symptoms presented in my teaching, although the depersonalization and cynicism toward students whom I had once lived for might have been the hardest part. For example, Lianne told me she had had a jump start on burnout going into graduate school after being a middle-school teacher for years. As a teacher's teacher in graduate school, she did what needed to be done to make sure students had the education they deserved, even if it meant commuting to multiple schools as an adjunct to teach and make enough money to finish her PhD work.

Part of the second aspect of burnout, cynicism and depersonalization, is disconnecting from the people that you care for professionally, which is common among burned-out healthcare workers and teachers. But for the contingent NTT faculty Bridget Lepore spoke with, the students were what kept them going.

One of the things that stands out when I think about my conversations with faculty is that they did not complain about teaching or the students, at least not as a contributor to burning out. Beyond some comments related to short-term, task-related burning out (related to grading and preparation, but with the expectation that things would change shortly as the rhythm of the semester took over), the faculty I spoke with considered the students their primary responsibility.

Faculty who had very heavy teaching loads actually told me that the students were why they had not burned out. One particular faculty member had chosen to be a college teacher because she wanted to see students succeed. She did not resent the students for needing assistance, nor the work involved in supporting them. In fact, the students were what kept her from burning out; she could focus on them and their needs because she had a clear goal and believed it was important.

Other faculty felt the same way: they had signed on for teaching, teaching was their vocation, and therefore students deserved their time and attention. While some NTTs mentioned the number of students in classes or the amount of grading—both conditions that tenure-track faculty discuss as stressful—there was rarely any evident frustration with teaching or the activities associated with teaching. Given that most NTTs are hired with a teaching focus in mind, it makes sense that they are invested in this part of the job.

Jennifer Snodgrass also found that students were ultimately the most important aspect of her career, which reshaped the path she thought she was on:

> In the fourth year of my tenure-track position, I found myself on eight different university committees, holding national leadership positions in both of my discipline societies, and advising two student organizations. I was on the "fast track" to become a chair or a dean. I was encouraged by my deans, colleagues, and friends to think seriously about a future in administration. The more I led meetings, found funding, or instigated change, the more I became sure of my future as an administrator in higher education.
>
> From the outside it looked as if I had it all, but the truth was that I was not really content. I lost sleep worrying about budgets, enrollment numbers, and faculty loads. Both my teaching and my research suffered because all of my time was invested in preparing for or directing meetings. I pushed all of this to the back of my mind; after all, I was going into administration, where I would only teach one class a semester, tops.
>
> I began to seriously think about leaving Appalachian State in my twelfth year. Institutions had been calling my office for several

years, requesting an application for teaching and administrative positions, but it never seemed to be the right time or fit. In the spring of 2016, I received the call that changed everything. The institution was looking for a new chair, and the search committee thought I was the "perfect candidate." This school was in my dream location and offered both traditional and commercial music degrees, an ideal fit with my own teaching and research agendas. When I went out to the interview, I knew that I wanted to take the position. I was ready for the challenge and eager to help start the conversation. The contract arrived two weeks after my interview, along with a sweatshirt bearing the school's logo and name. I've never felt more wanted or valued.

The contract was sitting on my desk when I went to the end-of-semester awards celebration at Appalachian. I was set to be the first presenter and give out an award for student leadership. When I walked out on the stage, all four hundred students in attendance began cheering loudly. I paused and looked out at the audience and realized in that moment that I wasn't done at Appalachian. I certainly was not ready to quit teaching and mentoring undergraduates. And I knew in that instant that I was not in love with the idea of becoming an administrator. Those students saved me that day from what I feel would have been a tremendous mistake.

An hour after that celebration, I called the institution and turned down the job. I immediately went to my dean and asked to alter my schedule. It was incredibly important that I get back to the moments that made me fall in love with my field. I asked for a sabbatical to start a large writing project and requested that I be removed from the majority of university committees. He agreed to all of these, and that night I slept better than I had in a very long time. I didn't know it, but I was burned out. All the signs were there, but I chose to ignore them. I had lost sleep, begun to talk poorly about others and myself, and found myself dreading each and every meeting. The higher up I went in administration, the more I realized the dangers of power to the psyche, others' and my own. It was not a healthy environment for me, but I was so busy listening to everyone telling me what I should do that I ignored what I wanted to do. Somehow, I had let other people's thoughts on my future dictate my path. I needed to find my original purpose.

I credit the students in the awards assembly and my 8:00 a.m. first-year class for helping me rediscover that purpose. Removing myself from all the service responsibilities for one semester did wonders for my overall well-being. I was able to hold all my office hours and talk more with my students one-on-one. I began to mentor my junior colleagues and to have honest conversations about curriculum design and effective teaching. I found the time and inspiration to write and finish a book about effective teaching. And my skills in motivation, delegation, and organization, strengthened in leadership roles, have proven to be just as important in the classroom and in the smaller, departmental committees on which I now serve. I have realized that my main purpose in my academic life is in the classroom. I still serve on committees and still encourage change, but the track of higher administration is no longer the holy grail for my academic journey. I still have small burnout moments, but I am able to pull myself out of the fire quickly before I am consumed.

It's important to find your purpose and a way to remind yourself of it. After I made the decision to focus on teaching rather than moving into full-time administration, I covered my piano with pictures of former students. This is my reminder of why I focus so much on my work in the classroom. I have quotes from famous musicians and authors on my door and wall to keep me in check. The quote "Successful people are not gifted; they just work hard and succeed on purpose" greets me on my office door every morning, reminding me to work diligently toward my goals. And my board in my office is covered with drawings from my daughter, mostly so that my students can see that it is possible to blend parenthood and a successful career. My current professional life purpose may be best summed up in a quote from Dolly Parton: "If your actions create a legacy that inspires others to dream more, learn more, do more and become more, then you are an excellent leader."

Committing to Social Justice

While working toward social justice has long been part of the mission of many institutions, what that looks like in practice can often be murky. The #MeToo movement, LGBTQIA rights work, and extensive protests following the murders of Armaud Arbery, Breonna Taylor, and George Floyd, among many other events before and during the COVID-19 pandemic, have brought diversity, equity, and inclusion (DEI) initiatives rightfully to the fore. Many women faculty members I spoke with were involved in social justice work with their students and communities, and although they were sometimes discouraged by the sheer volume of challenges and emotional labor, they found the work grounding, important, and purposeful.

The coach, lawyer, and PhD Michelle Dionne Thompson, for example, finds joy with her clients who are doing meaningful and important research:

The clients I work with that are the most pleasurable have had these groundbreaking projects. I've worked with Indigenous women, and one woman wrote her dissertation on the impacts of marijuana cultivation on Indigenous communities because it's damaging the water and salmon runs. These are the women I love to work with the most because they're really imbued with that sense of purpose, community, spirit, if you will, and knowledge. The clients who have those kinds of projects that combine those things together make my heart sing.

Several of the faculty women of color with whom I spoke acknowledged the additional emotional labor and work associated with being the only or one of the few Black, Brown, or Indigenous women in their department, or even in their institution. Whether they intended it or not, social justice became a core part of their work with students within and outside the classroom. For example, Valentina, who had completed her postdoc in the same lab where she now worked on one-year contracts, was told that she would be running diversity initiatives within the department as part of her load because, even though she was working at a minority-serving institution, she was the only woman of color in the department and therefore assumed to be interested in and qualified to run those initiatives. But when the initiatives didn't materialize, she decided to push for them: "No one else was doing it, and I realized it was an area where I could make a difference to students, something I could do on my own even though I was on yearly contracts."

Additionally, of the women faculty members I spoke with who identified as queer, one found themselves mentoring large numbers of minority-identifying students. For example, as the only queer-presenting faculty member in the small university's STEM college, Chris found themselves counseling students every day, intentionally or not. For a person who taught and studied theoretical mathematics, this was not a role they were comfortable with, but they took it on, remembering how important this type of mentoring had been to them when they were in college. Many conversations Chris had were with students who were not even in their classes but who needed help processing racism at the university or their own PTSD, survivor's guilt, depression, or suicidal ideations. Chris became closely connected with student life and knew the resources available to these students but still felt a responsibility to be there for them, despite the toll it was beginning to take on their own wellness and mental health.

Other faculty members spoke of social justice work in terms of supporting student advocacy on campus, addressing student poverty and food scarcity at their institutions, working with the community on issues like high incarceration rates and lack of access to health care via service-learning projects in their courses, and creating antiracist and antibullying efforts. And while each faculty member was deeply committed to these social justice efforts, it's easy to burn out from this additional emotional labor, and many were still dealing with this tension.

Work Outside Academia

Although teaching and social justice work helped faculty understand and address burnout not everyone finds their purpose inside the academy. Here are two examples as told by Sharon Mitchler:

After working for many years in business administration, Lauren completed a doctoral degree in art history. At 36, she was teaching two introductory classes as an adjunct at two separate colleges, and a lot of her time was taken up with commuting. Lauren felt burnt out, guilty, tired, and trapped. She knew she was supposed to feel privileged to work in her chosen field since teaching positions in art history that paid enough to make a living were few and far between. However, in her role as an adjunct she was beginning to question whether she was creating anything of value with her work.

Lauren wasn't sure whether she wanted to keep pursuing an academic career or go back to working in business. I asked what drew her to art history. Embarrassed, she said, "I just loved the beauty of the objects." When I asked what was embarrassing about that, she said, "It seems to me the field is less about explaining historical context or the creation of art now, and instead revolves around a critique of social stratification and the role of money in art collection." As we talked, she said, "You know, I think I might like to sign up for a class on making jewelry." Lauren settled on a four-hour beginning silversmith class.

She then expanded the time devoted to attending jewelry classes. She laughed about how her hobby had become more consuming than her teaching work, but she became certain that she was going to stop teaching art history at the end of the semester. From this modest beginning, Lauren was able to set up a business for herself in which she made use of all her skills: she opened a studio to design and make her own jewelry and teach classes. She uses her knowledge of ancient smithing techniques to teach, and she designs "arty" jewelry she hopes "will stand the test of time." She uses her business administration skills to keep the classes profitable enough to support herself. Her time in academia prepared her for this wonderful third career.

Madison graduated in 2014 with an MFA and taught on and off until 2018. But she never taught the same class twice. She taught only one class on a campus she had been to before, and she never had a contract that lasted longer than a single semester. At one college, she wasn't even allowed to use the copy machine because, as she was told, she was not faculty.

At one point, Madison interviewed to replace the only humanities professor on a satellite campus of an R1. They gave her an eleven-page list of subjects and classes that ranged from art, history, and gender and sexuality studies to music, literature, and world languages and indicated that the more classes she was willing to teach, the stronger her candidacy would be. But she spent most of the interview explaining to hard-science faculty that in creative fields like fine arts, making work and planning exhibitions was the intellectual work, not publishing articles or presenting at conferences. She did not get the job.

So in early 2019 Madison decided to invest the time and energy she was spending pursuing a career in higher ed into her personal art practice. The goal was to earn the money she would have made by teaching through selling artwork. By the end of the calendar year she had made more money selling her art on Instagram than she had made in all the semesters she'd spent teaching combined (which, she says, was not hard given that she'd been teaching as an adjunct). In 2020, despite the pandemic, maternity leave, and life as the mother of a newborn, she cleared $60,000 in art sales and was confident a six-figure revenue was possible within the next eighteen months.

For Madison, "small business owner" was a better title than "professor," and, ultimately, having her own business made it possible to pay off student loans and own a home. Lauren sometimes wonders what her graduate program would say about her nonacademic accomplishments and feels like a failure for leaving academia, but as the distance grows, it's easier to forget what mattered to higher ed. She is happier now carving her own path.

Artists are certainly not the only ones with terminal degrees to leave the academic work force. In my work and network, I've met women turning their degrees and experience into successful coaching, consulting, facilitation, and speaking businesses, some full-time and some as side hustles. They run yoga studios, accounting firms, and research programs. Many still work with faculty at all career stages: graduate students; early-, mid-, and late-career faculty; administrators and new leaders; and even those transitioning out of higher ed. They run writing retreats and group programs, keynote on important faculty development topics, and develop online courses on pedagogy, career change, and productivity strategies. They write faculty development books, supporting faculty in all manner of career and personal choices. They use their skills and talents to support faculty in unique and personal ways that empower them to move past burnout and do their most meaningful work.

For seventeen years, I, like Lianne, was a teacher's teacher, with the twin driving purposes of student success and learning and professional advancement. In my case, burnout shifted those goals and reshaped them into work I now see adjacent to the original motivators. I left my role as a tenured professor to work with faculty exclusively; I see my role now as that of a faculty member who helps peers and colleagues be the best teachers and mentors they can be. In terms of using my skills outside academia as well, at the time of this writing I'm working toward my coaching certification, focusing on meaningful productivity, writing skills, career development, and burnout resilience. I'm also dabbling in developmental editing with book authors, a skill born of my extensive writing and editing experience and direct work with hundreds of academic and scholarly writers. And I've created a group coaching program about burnout resilience based on this book. I say this to show how our skills and talents are often (more) valued in other contexts.

Each faculty member whose story contributed to this chapter is following their own paths to (re)find and (re)articulate their purposes in the context of burnout, whether impending or current. Each experience is unique, each person finding their own way, each brave in their efforts to claim their driving purpose for their own.

Reflection Opportunity

- What do you love to do more than anything else, in general and in higher ed?
- What do you regret not doing in your career so far? What's keeping you from doing it?
- What would it take for you to pursue your purpose?

Conclusion

As I conducted the research for this book, I was struck by the tension between doing work that faculty find fulfilling and purposeful and taking care of one's mental, physical, and emotional health. Each woman I spoke with craved meaningful work and the opportunity to make a difference in the students' lives and in her discipline, institution, and community. And part of that work was separating out the purpose and values of each woman from the purpose and values of her higher ed context. For some that meant spending deeply reflective time (re)articulating their purpose and goals; for others, homing in on their work with students for social justice. Many acknowledged the emotional and cognitive load of doing their work in higher ed, especially when there was a disconnect between their purpose-driven goals and those of academia writ large.

REVISITING YOUR PURPOSE, YOUR MISSION

Now that you've thought about your values, purpose, and sense of meaning, revise or create a few purpose statements that reflect what you care about now—not what higher ed cares about but what you as a person and a professional care about. Consider these questions as you reflect on your purpose statements:

- Are the statements you wrote aligned with your own values or higher ed's (or both)?
- What are you doing when you feel most aligned with your purpose?
- Which of your values is most important to your purpose?
- What can you do to be more aligned with your values and purpose?

When I entered my PhD program, I did so to escape what I thought was failure in the world outside academia. And after seventeen years of taking higher ed's purpose and priorities as my own, burnout was the wake-up call I needed to take stock, reassess, and recommit to values and a purpose that worked for me, which meant life changes and a career shift toward work that I saw as more meaningful for me at the time. Following our purposes and committing to values is an important part of the process of warding off and overcoming burnout.

CHAPTER 4

Compassion

I don't think I would have told anyone on campus about my burnout and mental-health struggle if I hadn't had a panic attack in front of a senior colleague two weeks before the fall semester of 2018. I dreaded a new semester, and a misunderstanding about my schedule had led to one of my first-year writing classes meeting twice in the first week but the second meeting only once, meaning they would be out of sync until fall break in October. Given my mental state, this schedule, which should have been merely annoying, felt disastrous. So in early August I shakingly resigned myself to this nightmare and went to campus to pick up the textbooks I needed, catastrophizing and ruminating all the way there.

As soon as I walked toward my building, my chest seized up, and I knew I had to grab the books, avoid everyone, and get out fast if I didn't want to have a breakdown. But as fate would have it, one of my senior colleagues was in her office. She greeted me warmly and asked me the question I feared most in the world: "How was your summer?" Hopeless, I tried to explain my calamitous schedule for the fall and began to have a panic attack as I spoke, hyperventilating, lungs in a vice.

Because this was so out of character for me, she was necessarily alarmed. I managed to get out that I was being treated for burnout, depression, and anxiety and felt ashamed for freaking out in my own office, which just made me hyperventilate more, of course.

In that moment, her compassion saved me. She spoke kindly but firmly, maintaining eye contact. She said that I had been so productive, a model departmental and university citizen, for so long that I absolutely deserved a break to cope with my burnout. She strongly advised me to email the department chair about the schedule immediately. With her practically standing over my shoulder, I emailed our department chair asking to speak with her about my mental-health concerns going into the semester. And then I shut my office door and cried.

Eventually I called my husband, who talked me down and out of my office to drive home. The audio track in my head just kept asking how I could possibly go to work if I had a panic attack every time I walked into my office or cried every time someone asked me about my summer. As I drove, I admitted to myself that it wasn't just the classes that terrified me; it was all my projects and responsibilities—the service commitments, articles and book projects, journal special issue, new major ramp-up, pilot program assessment. I had bought into higher ed's mentality that we are only as good as our productivity, so I thought these projects were necessary if I was to get the attention, respect, prestige, and next-level leadership roles I deserved.

Laura and my psychiatrist had told me repeatedly that I needed to step back from as much as possible at work until I could get a handle on my emotional burnout. I pushed back at them both: there was no possible way I could let everyone else down by forcing my work on them. I was the leader these projects needed, and no one else. But I also knew that someone else *could* do my work, and do it so well that I would be easily replaceable. Without those projects keeping me in front of important people, I would be forgotten and left behind. Surely I would miss my shot at earning an award or promotion or anything that proved my excellence.

Looking back, my deepest fear was to go unnoticed professionally since my work was my life. I was afraid to admit I was human, not superhuman, in higher education. And I would never have told anyone about my struggle, let alone asked for help, if it hadn't been for my colleague's compassion, and that of my department chair, in one of my scariest, most vulnerable moments. Even though I didn't want it or feel like I deserved it, their kindness and understanding probably saved me in the long run. And they modeled a new way to think about myself as a person in higher ed. Or maybe outside it.

Reflection Opportunity

- What does compassion look like to you?
- How are you currently practicing compassion toward others and yourself?
- How does compassion practice align with your values and purpose?

Why Are We Talking about Compassion?

Compassion wasn't something I thought much about in general, let alone in relation to my role as a faculty member and scholar. I had cultivated an outward performance of myself as intimidating or strong; and intimidating, strong faculty members don't walk around throwing hugs at people like candy. Thinking back, I don't remember hearing gossip about people burning out or going down in flames, though I know now it did happen, but if I had, I'm sure I would have outwardly lamented their misfortunate while silently judging them for not being able to hack it. I was clearly better than they were. It wasn't until my own experience with burnout, shattering my assumptions about everything, that compassion became part of my vocabulary. It became something I needed from others and needed to give myself.

Professions demanding regular empathy, caring, and emotional presence, like healthcare, social work, and teaching, are likely to see a higher incidence of burnout and compassion fatigue than other professions (Maslach, Schaufeli, and Leiter 2001; Teven 2007). Good teachers build personal relationships with students that are grounded in looking out for their welfare; students know teachers care about them when we exhibit empathy, understanding, and responsiveness to their needs (Teven 2007, 383). But sustaining high levels of empathy—imagining what someone else is going through—and maintaining wells of compassion from which we recognize and want to relieve stress or fear in others is exhausting (Hanson and Hanson 2018, 9; Schwartz and Sharpe 2010, 23).

Exhaustion, the first hallmark of burnout, is not just the feeling we have after a long week or after surviving the dreaded month of April. When tenured or tenure-track faculty say we're exhausted at those times, coming from our place of privilege, we often wear that exhaustion as a badge of honor, a nod to our selfless workaholism, rather than an invitation for help and caring from others. The exhaustion I'm talking about here is bone deep. It's a physical, emotional, and intellectual emptiness; you have nothing left to give, especially to yourself, because you are completely overextended and under constant strain (Maslach, Schaufeli, and Leiter 2001, 399). It's the exhaustion felt by many adjuncts, contract faculty, and faculty of color so much more than tenured or tenure-track faculty.

Minoritized faculty often experience the exhaustion in very different ways than white, straight faculty members, as they take on far more compassionate and emotional labor with minoritized students. Tiana, a popular non-tenure-track humanities professor of color shared,

> I feel tired all the time. There's a heaviness that I carry that my colleagues who aren't of color don't have to, an awareness of the suffering of our student body, our students of color, international students, LGBTQIA students, who don't see a lot of people like them. I carry the weight with me of that awareness about my own body moving in the world, but also about our students. And there's just not that awareness there for a lot of my colleagues. Of course, they're sympathetic, and they want their students to do well, but those students aren't having the same conversations with them that they are with me. My spouse is a white straight man in a different department. There are things I'll talk about, and he's like, I'm not aware of that. And these are students that we share sometimes. But yeah, it's like a physical weight, and I'm slowly realizing that other people do not carry the same weight.

Jane Jones, a sociologist and coach who works with academics especially in the area of writing, explains the burden of that emotional labor carried by minoritized faculty:

> Just the feeling that there's really no one you can ask for help because they won't understand the specific type of help you need, and you're often the only Black person in your department. Other people just don't understand why that joke wasn't funny or why you shouldn't be mentoring all of these students at one time. And students don't understand it either. They see the one Black person in the department, and everyone wants to be mentored by them. But you can't mentor twelve-plus people this semester. So, there's this whole level of having to, but you just can't. And you also can't say "students want to work with me

because I'm Black" to other people. So that is definitely like an enduring struggle.

Although I cannot possibly understand the additional pressures laid upon faculty of color and from marginalized groups, the way I had set myself up as a professor and mentor did lead to more emotional engagement than was healthy for me personally. Learning how to feel and demonstrate compassion for others and to make compassion toward myself a daily practice helped me to develop burnout resilience and hope. Brené Brown (2017) says that compassion, along with courage and connection, helps us to see and know ourselves as *enough* (xix), which was certainly one of the drivers of my overwork and overcommitment to higher ed values, both positive and not so positive ones. To really believe I was enough, and for the other women whose stories I share here to believe that they were enough, we had to deal with our emotional exhaustion, the shame that came from it, and the gaslighting we had experienced to get to a place of self-compassion and to really see ourselves as whole people outside academia.

The faculty member and yoga instructor Tiffany D. Johnson offers a way to gift yourself compassionate awareness:

> About five years ago, I was in the final year of my doctoral program and on the job market, splitting my time between interviews, school visits, and my dissertation. I had learned to incorporate monthly massages into my routine due to prior health concerns related to overworking. My massage therapist had seen me consistently, almost monthly, over the past four years. She was accustomed to my habits and knew what my body felt like when it was nearing burnout. One day, she could feel in my body that I was exhausted and on the verge. She advised—actually, begged—me to go

home, drink lots of water, and not touch my work until the next day (Monday).

I took her advice. Some inner voice, inner wisdom, nudged me, told me not to work even that night, not to touch that laptop, and not to try to edit that PowerPoint presentation. Her words of wisdom stick with me to this day as an inner knowing, an inner teacher, if you will.

We can learn so much from a consistent practice of awareness, of compassionate witnessing toward others and toward ourselves. Such witnessing can help us to slow down, resist burnout, and still do the work we love to do. As a yoga instructor, I often lead my classes in this type of reflection. Here are two meditations you can use to practice compassionate witnessing for yourself.

Short Exercise on Being Witnessed: Reflection Questions / Journaling Prompts

Mini-meditation 1. Come to a space in your home or favorite place that is most comfortable for you. Bring with you a journal, a pen or pencil, and perhaps a hot beverage. To begin, reflect on these questions:

- What does "meaningfulness" mean to you?
- What are some tasks in your academic work that are meaningful to you?
- When was the last time you felt energetic, that is, full of emotional, cognitive, and/or physical energy? What are some thought processes, behaviors that you engaged in?

After you answer these questions, close your eyes if that is comfortable for you, and notice your inhales and exhales. After one or two minutes of noticing your breath, bring awareness to what sensations arise in your body, if any, as you consider these thought processes and behaviors. Where do you feel them? Perhaps you place your hand over that area while you breathe in silence for two more minutes. If your eyes are closed, open them and move on to the next reflection prompt.

Mini-meditation 2. Reflect upon the last time you felt drained, overworked, and/or low in emotional, cognitive, and/or physical energy. What are some thought processes, behaviors that you engaged in?

Bonus journaling. Write down one or two ways that you can practice being a witness unto yourself today while you are at work and three to five things you are grateful for before you close your journal for the day.

May this be useful to you as you engage in the very important work that you do in academia so much so that you become not only a consistent and compassionate witness of your needs for rest and relaxation but also a compassionate witness for colleagues and fellow students with similar needs.

What about Compassion Fatigue and Exhaustion?

Just as I didn't think much about compassion before burnout, I've never thought of myself as a particularly emotional person. I used to cry if someone forced me to sit through a sad movie about animals like *The Lion King,** but otherwise I'm pretty stoic. And when it came to students, I was pretty patient—I didn't put up with crap, but I tried to be encouraging. It was when those things started to change, and when

---

* I was deeply scarred by Baloo's non-death in *The Jungle Book* and by a grade-school viewing of *Old Yeller*.

I cried at the drop of a hat and could only roll my eyes at student needs, that I could have admitted something was wrong.

I see now that these are classic signs of both emotional exhaustion and depersonalization, the kind of deep exhaustion that drains your physical, intellectual, and emotional self. In the case of workplace burnout, those feelings become chronic, and I didn't have much left to give to students or to other aspects of my faculty role (Maslach, Jackson, and Leiter 1996; Sabagh, Hall, and Saroyan 2018). The standard emotional labor with students that had once been professionally satisfying became debilitating and anxiety-producing. Adding students' needs to my own just led to compassion fatigue, random crying spells, and shame that I wasn't who I thought I was.

Brené Brown (2012) says that "emotional accessibility is a shame trigger for researchers and academics. Very early in our training, we are taught that a cool distance and inaccessibility contribute to prestige, and that if you're too relatable, your credentials come into question" (12). In a culture that does not suffer weakness very well, many faculty, especially women, may manage emotions in unhealthy ways, attempting to seem more positive than we feel or to pretend to be fine when in reality we are being dragged under by frustration and dissatisfaction (Stupnisky, Hall, and Pekrun 2019a, 1493–94; Teven 2007, 384). Audrey, a faculty member who left academia for several years, told me,

> I was in a really messy situation while doing my PhD, trying to juggle classes and writing, a long-distance relationship, and, because I didn't have funding, a full-time job that kept me away from campus most of the time. That time really established for me the messed-up idea that I just need to get through this right now and later I'll be able to remedy the impacts to my physical and mental health. But I couldn't do it just then. I was never doing things that would keep me healthy. Just working.

Leaving academia for a few years was ultimately necessary to getting her mental and physical health under control away from the toxic environment(s) that caused the unhealthy behaviors.

In my case, I did everything I could to pretend I was doing well during the second year of the design-thinking studio pilot program, which sped me into burnout. Since the students in the first cohort had labeled me cold and unforgiving, I was the exact opposite in the second iteration. I was perky, lighthearted, flexible, and emotionally available, even though it took a deep toll on my mental health . . . and didn't seem to work very well with them.

When we do this, in the classroom, in the lab, or in an advising session, we often don't see compassion fatigue as a warning sign, but I knew I was exhausted. According to Maslach, Schaufeli, and Leiter (2001), "Exhaustion is not something that is simply experienced—rather, it prompts actions to distance oneself emotionally and cognitively from one's work, presumably as a way to cope with the overload" (403). When your professional identity depends on the messages you get from the culture around you, true exhaustion is to be hidden.

Maya experienced these feelings of exhaustion and found compassion from an unexpected group when she shared her struggle.

I teach at an institution that is having issues right now with institutional transparency, responsibility, and communication. Our salaries are public record, and after browsing one day, I realized that a male colleague of mine in my area who had been there for six years fewer than me was making almost twelve thousand dollars more than me. When I approached the dean to discuss this, I was told first that it was because of the tenure salary bump and then that it was because he had a retention offer; I had also had both. My dean then told me I was performing below expectations, when my yearly evaluation show I'm a productive scholar and an effective teacher.

At the same time, a student had a violent outburst in my class-room, to the point where my graduate assistant and I were afraid of him. While trying to follow the proper channels to report this inci-dent, I realized that the university had no mechanism in place to handle these issues. Each university office I contacted passed me along to someone else, and the only action that was offered was by a police detective who offered to bring the student in and "scare him into acting right" in my classroom. (I declined that offer.)

These two things seem unrelated, but the combination made me feel unappreciated, unrecognized, and unsupported (financially and emotionally). I spiraled into burnout and depression and after a semester basically gave up. I was completely burned out, completely unproductive, completely behind, and I didn't see a way out. I inves-tigated taking a medical leave for mental-health reasons. I seriously considered just quitting my tenured job entirely. Unsurprisingly, my personal life was also suffering. I felt like I couldn't do the right thing in any aspect of my life, either professional or personal.

While I was in that burnout/depression, I realized at one point that I hadn't graded projects my graduate class had turned in a month earlier. At the next weekly course meeting, I saw no other way to handle the situation than to tell them what was going on. I admitted to them that I was depressed and that I was having trou-ble functioning. I told them truthfully that the time I spent in the classroom with them was what kept me going because I loved their enthusiasm, which made me feel like myself again.

I'm not sure what I thought would happen, but the students were completely supportive. We spent almost an hour of our semi-nar talking about how academia dissuades people from talking about mental health and how everyone feels that they need to appear fine, all the time. The students acknowledged that they had felt that way at some point and that they understood what I was going through. I actually started crying at one point in front of my students because the conversation made me realize how heavily this had been weighing on me for so long.

After that class, quite a few of the students came to talk to me individually about their own mental-health issues, and several of them checked in on me regularly throughout the rest of the semester. I got more support from my students than I did from my colleagues, my administration, or my institution.

What's happened since? I finally admitted that I needed help. I went to a psychiatrist, who put me on a low dose of an antidepressant, which seems to help with both the depression and burnout and the complete lack of focus. I also started talking openly about mental health within academia, both within my area and within my college, and on social media. I now feel like it's my mission to help graduate students and young faculty members normalize talking about how the pressure of academia affects us. My colleague still makes more than I do. But some of my graduate students from that course continue to check in on me, and I on them.

Sometimes support comes from really unexpected places.

Reflection Opportunity

- What does exhaustion look like to you?
- What was a time you felt emotionally exhausted at work? How did you deal with that?

- What strategies do you use to cope with exhaustion? What about those strategies is, or is not, working for you?
- In what ways might exhaustion and compassion fatigue impact those around you?

Thoughts on Gaslighting and Depersonalizing

Emotional exhaustion can often come from a misalignment between our core values and the cultural values and activities we take for granted in higher ed. While we value lifelong learning and liberal* ideals as faculty, we also get sucked into the driving expectation escalation, competition, and the never-ending quest for high achievement. As I've researched burnout, I started to see some of those underlying cultural values and the behaviors they generate as gaslighting. In their work on women and burnout, Nagoski and Nagoski (2019) explain that "gaslighting is designed to make you question your own credibility and competence.... The message is strong—whatever is wrong it's your fault.... You haven't tried hard enough. You haven't done the right things. You don't have what it takes. Eventually what can we do but believe them?" (86).

The messages I took in from higher ed, and sometimes from peers and colleagues, about being an endlessly productive, intellectual life role model without any perceivable weakness made me feel, at the risk of being hyperbolic, doomed as I slipped farther into depression, anxiety, and burnout. I got the messages from all around me, locally and beyond, as I tried to avoid disappointing people, which always seemed right around the corner. The story I began to tell myself was that I was a fraud, weak, useless—and that I had to hide at all costs. Self-compassion was not something I was used to. Part of it probably was gaslighting

* In the classical sense, not the current political sense.

about the double binds of being a competent professional woman in a culture that expects women faculty to be strong but soft, compassionate but not emotional, leaders but not "in charge." And in higher ed, we need external approval for just about everything we are trained to want, such as promotion and tenure, publication or conference acceptances, departmental course assignments, etc. If anyone knew how I felt, my career, and so my life, would be over. No one directly told me any of those things, but my inner critic, or maybe my inner Reviewer 2, wouldn't let up.

Lee Skallerup Bessette experienced this gaslighting most of her life, until a diagnosis helped her defeat the gaslighting narrative and control her burnout:

> When I was growing up, I heard two comments about myself constantly: "What is wrong with you?" and "You're so lazy!" But I didn't know I had ADHD when I was a child; I was a smart kid who just needed to "apply herself and stop acting weird." Women are often overlooked for ADHD because we typically manifest the symptoms differently: girls get lost in their own heads. I was also called a "space cadet" a lot as a kid. So, I kept trying harder to please, and I kept burning out. I would beat myself up over missed deadlines or missed parties and social events or poor performances that let people down. I would often go into a shame spiral because I was so overcommitted and couldn't do everything well enough or consistently enough for everyone's liking or standards.
>
> Fast forward, and a PhD can be a dangerous place for someone with ADHD because it is all so new and so stimulating and for the first time you can do what you want, what interests you. But you can quickly get overwhelmed trying to make all of the various masters of the academy happy. I still felt lazy and like I wasn't trying

hard enough. I tried a faculty role but needed something different, so I changed careers and found that alt-ac work played to my strengths. It was social, collaborative, always changing, always new, never routine, and played to my strong knowledge base. It was suddenly a good thing that I was interested in a lot of things! And yet, I still wasn't working up to "my potential," and I was still being asked, albeit in a more professional way, "What is wrong with you?"

It wasn't until my son was diagnosed with ADHD and I started reading about it that I realized that that was what was "wrong" with me. It explained so much about how I worked, how I reacted, how I behaved, how I processed the world, and why I didn't make sense to anyone else. It was a relief. I had worked so hard my entire life to be what everyone else wanted me to be (a.k.a. neurotypical) that I kept burning out and falling into depressive episodes. When I got a proper diagnosis, I could finally let go of everyone else's expectations of me, embrace who I am, finally explain what I was thinking and feeling.

I am much more aware of my patterns and why they happen and when I need to pull back, without guilt or apology now. I'm learning how to manage my energy, to observe rather than judge my reactions, to be kinder and more compassionate to myself than I have ever been. I try to model that kindness and that grace and understanding to my friends and colleagues, but especially to my children, who both have ADHD as well. I am more aware and attuned to myself and my needs, and I am now OK with asking for what I need, as well as negotiating compromises, rather than trying to compromise myself.

I think the biggest reason I regularly burned out was the exhaustion from trying to be neurotypical. I could still burn out because my ADHD can run me into the ground with an endless list of new and exciting things I could be and end up saying yes to doing. But now I say yes not because I'm worried someone will think I'm lazy if I say no but because I actually want to.

Perfectionism, imposter syndrome, and chronic overachieving seem to be common concerns for many academic women, derived from the cultural and personal messages we receive about how we should be in the world. As I noted in chapter 2, coach Katie Linder told me that nearly every woman in higher ed that she has worked with had imposter syndrome or something similar. She talked about these women being surprised that everyone had these feelings, because "no one ever talks about it." Of course they don't. A junior faculty woman in a study by Hutchins and Rainbolt (2017) sums this up well: "These are the kinds of things that we don't really talk about because I think we feel what we feel. I don't know if the right word is ashamed, but that is very private (and) you don't want to tell other people that you're unsure of yourself or that you don't think you can live up to the expectations (of the job)" (206).

And even when institutions provide resources to cope with these perspectives, faculty may not access them for reasons of "confidentiality and fear of being exposed" (Hutchins and Rainbolt 2017, 207). But exposed as what? weak? vulnerable? human? The mental-health advocate for graduate students Susanna Harris shared how she connects gaslighting to higher education:

> If you follow the pace of academia, like flat out, if you follow what is expected of you, you are going to burn out because what is expected of you is impossible; it's almost gaslighting. The conversation needs to shift from how to not be a "bad" grad student, or how to not let grad school crush you, to just how to be a grad student who can recognize when you need to refill yourself and not break down.

Assuming the graduate student is coming to me saying, "I'm totally burnt out," I usually start the conversation with empathy, saying, "This is the situation you're in. It's not your fault; there's no fault at this. Let's just start it from here. Let's just accept that things are not good right now." And we take a look at what we might be able to do to make things a little bit better, remembering it's really important to help the grad student know they shouldn't feel guilty for needing help.

I'm asking questions like "Is this how you want to be living? Is this how you want to be feeling? Look at your days, look at how you're feeling week by week—is this how you want to be as a person?" Almost always they will say, "No, but I have no choice." So, I usually say, "Okay, we're not negating anything. Let's say maybe you don't have a choice right now, but we can work to what you actually want to have, breaking it down into whys: why you're feeling what you're feeling, why you're not living the life that you want to, why you're stressed again."

Actually, adding the extra effort of combating a burnout is asking them to do additional work, but it will pay out in the long run. We talk about ways that they think they might feel burned out way less, what actions have to be done, and who can keep them accountable to do them. And that's usually where we branch into the mental health, too. We might talk about the fact that people with no history of mental illness can absolutely burn out. People with existing mental illness are more likely to, and there are more likely to be ongoing complications, but one is not the other. It's really hard to tease the two out. So the point is that the label is useful but not necessary. You can call it burnout. You can call it a bad year. Call it whatever you want, but it's about, are you happy living the way that you're living? Or do you want to change? Do you want to be living this way in a month? And that's what we work on.

You could plug in *faculty member* for *grad student* and Harris's point remains accurate. When we feel exposed, we develop coping strategies to protect ourselves, our egos, our self-esteem, and our sense of belonging or placeness (Westerman et al. 2016, 66). Depersonalization is a major symptom of burnout and a pretty effective, if dysfunctional, coping strategy. When you depersonalize, you put distance between yourself and the people you serve because it's easier to work or manage when you see them impersonally (Maslach, Schaufeli, and Leiter 2001, 403).

Compassion fatigue often manifests through depersonalization, or even before. The symptoms include "checking out emotionally, minimizing or dismissing suffering that isn't the most extreme; feeling helpless, hopeless, powerless, while also feeling personally responsible for doing more; [and] staying in a bad situation" (Nagoski and Nagoski 2019, 95–96).

Over time, it got so I didn't have anything left to give to my students, which was ironic considering my need to be needed. And the more burned out I grew, the more my ability to cope with students, colleagues, and my reactions to them frayed (see Brown 2017, 189). My compassion fatigue was a coping mechanism, as Maslach, Schaufeli, and Leiter (2001) state, speaking specifically here about nonacademic workplaces: "Moderating one's compassion for clients by emotional distance from them ('detached concern') was viewed as a way of protecting oneself from intense emotional arousal that could interfere with functioning effectively on the job. However, an imbalance of excessive detachment and little concern seemed to lead staff to respond to clients in negative, callous, and dehumanizing ways" (400).

I didn't notice my compassion fatigue growing because, as I mentioned, I'm not an overly emotional person in general, but I knew I was putting distance between myself and my students and colleagues, which for me was out of character. I still regularly see idealistic pre-RPR me pop up in Facebook memories, exalting my students' cleverness or proclaiming that, above any campus politics, I knew I belonged in the classroom. I see those posts now and think, "oh, honey. . . ."

While I never thought of my students in "dehumanizing ways" even in the depths of burnout, I did start to see them as a collective rather than as individuals, and that alone was exhausting. I also see this online in other faculty members. I was careful to keep my thoughts about students to myself, but I continue to see faculty using Twitter especially to berate or mock students for some perceived deficiency or generational trope. The obsessive focusing on student cheating during remote instruction because of COVID seems pathological as well. What if those faculty members are experiencing burnout but have no understanding or language for what is happening and thus lash out? It's easier to lash out than to deal with our emotions, especially in a context that demands everything for teaching and research.

Mary Beth found herself coping with her burnout and feeling overwhelmed, but two interactions with students helped her course-correct toward self-compassion.

"What we learn is more important than what they learn." Mary Rose O'Reilley (2005) gives us this sentence to ponder on page 70 of her slim book about burnout, titled *The Garden at Night*. It reminds me of how several students noticed my symptoms of burnout in pre-tenure years.

On the morning of September 11, 2001, I was walking to campus wearing dark sunglasses to hide my hangover. A student caught up to me and started chattering, "Did you hear about the plane flying into the Twin Towers?" I thought she was telling me a joke. I chuckled in anticipation of the punch line. "No, I haven't heard the one about the plane flying into the Twin Towers," I smiled. She said, "Yeah, and one crashed into the Pentagon. My dad works there. I can't get a signal on my phone. I gotta find a phone," and she ran off. Suddenly, I noticed the people around me talking on their phones—lots of gesticulating and wide eyes. I realized, in that moment, that whatever I was afraid of normally just exceeded the normal and that I wasn't up to the challenge of caring for all these students in pain, like the young woman whose father worked in the Pentagon. Instead of facing that reality, I later avoided it with more wine.

Another incident burned into my mind involved a group of students who showed that they noticed some symptoms of my burnout early one morning in the next year. One student came to my office representing ten other students who wanted to point out some glaring discrepancies in my teaching. As she was outlining the complaints, I broke into a sweat. She stopped midsentence and asked, "Have you been eating garlic?" I told her I had cooked some pad thai the night before. (I had also drunk two bottles of sake; I had woken up late and dashed to school without a shower.) She said, "It's a really strong smell."

Although I was mortified, I remember this particular event with gratitude. My student was honestly noticing the results of my attempts to combat my anxieties with food and wine, and my behavior was affecting my teaching, my students, and my personal life. I changed my approach to the course in that moment, but it would take another couple of years to fully face the root of my anxiety.

When I was finally able to get clear about how my fear, burnout, and resulting behaviors were affecting everyone around me, it was these memories of clear messages that rose to the surface. What I thought I had been hiding so well was transparent to those around me. What I learned from them began to transform me both professionally and personally. Medication, then meditation helped me understand how I was causing much of my own suffering. It was the compassion of these students, even if they didn't know they were offering it, that set me on a path to self-compassion.

Mary Beth was reminded by students to take care of herself and offer herself compassion rather than to use avoidant coping behaviors to handle her challenges. Hutchins and Rainbolt (2017) found that women faculty tended to use more positive, people-oriented coping methods like reaching out for support from others as well as noticing and improving their self-talk, while men faculty were more likely to avoid or cope negatively with unpleasant feelings (206). Practicing self-compassion, taking the time to regularly and honestly check in with ourselves with the same kindness we would offer others, is necessary to ward off or work through burnout.

Looking back, I now see that I sometimes behaved in ways that gaslit others, as well as moralized or looked down on others while trying to make myself feel better. Brown (2017) tells us, "The ego says, 'Feelings are for losers and weaklings.' Avoiding truth and vulnerability are critical. . . . The ego likes blaming, finding fault, making excuses, inflicting payback, and lashing out, all of which are ultimate forms of self-protection" (62). I regret my behavior and know it was self-preservation that likely hurt others.

I needed to build up my self-knowledge to examine how I was coping with burnout and then practice self-compassion. The psychologist Dina Gohar thinks acceptance and commitment therapy (ACT) can offer some advice here:

We think if we fixed the problem, then we fixed the stressor. But that underestimates the importance of dealing with the emotion, honestly.

There's only so much anxiety our bodies can physically take before we get into that freeze response too. Repeated cognitive distortions like catastrophizing and rumination burn you out. Recognizing the false alarms and not necessarily reacting to them is important.

That's where the acceptance and commitment therapy approach, which is based on a mindfulness approach, is really helpful. In the ACT model, you (1) accept your reactions and sit with them; (2) choose a direction based on your values; and (3) take some defined action.

I can have this emotion; it can be there. I can have depression with me, I can have anxiety there, but they are just passengers on my bus with me. Sometimes they do take control, and that's scary. But you can be the one that's driving. Just don't forget that you are the driver and are in control. It means that you're just not trying to constantly control what they're saying and doing. Let them be rowdy passengers, but they're in the back of your mind. Those negative thoughts can come up, but you don't have to necessarily pay attention to them. Just because I have the thought doesn't mean it's real or driving me. Sometimes you just have to acknowledge and have compassion for yourself through it: I'm having the thought, or the story I'm telling myself is XYZ. That distance can help you through it.

Why Is Self-Compassion So Important to Recovery?

The hardest lesson I learned through my burnout was how to treat myself with compassion. Even though we rarely talk to others we care about the way we speak to ourselves, shaming self-talk and negative ruminations can be hard habits to break. It took a long time to focus less on my self-esteem, which was based on my accomplishments and how others validated me, to compassionately think about myself as a human with flaws who would be OK in the long run and learn from negative experiences (Neff, Kirkpatrick, and Rude 2007; Neff and Vonk 2009).

Kristin Neff defines self-compassion, largely on the basis of the principles of Buddhism, as a state of "being kind and understanding toward oneself in instances of pain or failure rather than being harshly self-critical; perceiving one's experiences as part of the larger human experience rather than seeing them as isolating; and holding painful thoughts and feelings in mindful awareness rather than over-identifying with them" (Neff, Kirkpatrick, and Rude 2007, 139). One way to take this mindful approach is to acknowledge those voices in your mind that either criticize or support you—your inner critic and your inner mentor—when you want to work on your self-compassion (see the box).

At the height of burnout, just as I had no compassion left for my students, I had no compassion at all for myself; my inner critic ruled my thoughts. All I had was a crumbling ego. Ashamed, I was setting myself apart from everyone else who still had it all together. My self-talk seemed a never-ending onslaught of thoughts about my stupidity, weakness, and uselessness, all because my productivity had halted. I became more and more disconnected from my students, colleagues, and RPR. I began to actively resent colleagues who had roles or titles I was sure I deserved (but didn't actually want because of the associated workload). As Rachael O'Meara (2017) says in such an understated way, "Mental chatter often takes the form of things you tell yourself that are not in your best interest" (63).

Jane Jones told me she spends a good deal of her time with clients focusing on rethinking thoughts and emotions:

I spend time with them examining the thoughts and how our thoughts make us feel. Then we look at not whether those feelings are good or bad but do you want to have them for the duration? For example, sometimes you're going to have a thought, and it's going to make you feel disappointed, and that's okay. But do you want to feel disappointed for weeks? Because if you don't, then let's talk about changing the thought, so really thinking about empowering people to believe just because it went across your head, doesn't mean it's "real," right? Because academics' brains are our everything, if you can't trust your brain, that's terrifying. You have to have compassion for yourself and realize this negative story I have about myself and my brain; it's going to take a while to unravel it.

Without self-compassion and before I'd had enough therapy to be able to process my thoughts and emotions in the way Jones describes, I didn't have a positive sense of self because I was no longer achieving the goals I and academia had set for me. It wasn't until I did the (really) hard work of decoupling my professional self-esteem from my personal selfhood that I was able to practice self-compassion. For quite a while, I was not at a place where I could look beyond my self-esteem to begin even thinking about treating myself with compassion, which "is felt precisely when life is not going so well, allowing for greater resilience and stability regardless of particular outcomes" (Neff and Vonk 2009, 27). It also took some time before I could clearly see ways I was allowing myself to be treated that were not acceptable in my newfound clarity.

Self-compassion also requires self-care in a true sense, not as a buzzword. True self-care goes beyond bubble baths and a day off. One of the most crucial lessons I learned was how to take more compassionate care of myself, which did mean some splurges on massages and pedicures, but more importantly it meant getting regular therapy and coaching,

TAMING YOUR INNER CRITIC WITH YOUR INNER MENTOR

Humans often experience a negativity bias that makes it more likely that we will pay attention to negative aspects of a situation even when the positive outweigh them. The inner critic rules unless the inner mentor can take over. The inner critic is the voice inside your head that keeps your doubt and cognitive distortions, like catastrophizing, rumination, and all-or-nothing thinking, on a nonstop loop. Your inner mentor might be a cheerleader, encourager, or voice of reason that can overcome the critic.

Consider the following questions to get in tune with both your inner critic and your inner mentor:

- Think about your inner critic. What does it say to you? What tone of voice does it use? What does the voice sound like? Can you visualize the critic? Can you describe how it looks? What does the inner critic get from you that sustains it? Does it have a name?
- Now think about your inner mentor. This voice might be buried under the shame loops of the inner critic, but bring it to the surface. What does your inner mentor look like? sound like? Does it have a name? How does the mentor speak to you? What would your inner mentor say to your inner critic?

Naming and physically describing the critic and mentor might seem silly at first, but once you know what they look and sound like, you can use those images to change your self-talk to treat yourself with more self-compassion. My inner critic is RPR, though it used to be a more amorphous version of some grade-school teachers. I've done this activity with people who identified the critic as a furry monster, an old white male faculty member, different versions of themselves, or (sadly) family members. My inner mentor is a combination of Mrs. Whatsit, Mrs. Which, and Mrs. Who from *A Wrinkle in Time* (1963).

You can use these characters to "talk back" to your ruminations and catastrophizing thoughts and to treat yourself with more compassion.

journaling, not working at all hours, and ultimately making a big career change that was unexpected but right for my family and me.

Self-care and self-compassion aren't necessarily synonymous with self-indulgence, but they do mean not assuming that pushing yourself with negative self-talk or letting others push you will keep you motivated or that taking breaks for rest and rejuvenation will put you more and more behind (Hanson and Hanson 2018, 173; Nagoski and Nagoski 2019, 211). Self-compassion is about giving yourself grace and understanding from a mindful and objective position (Hallett 2018, 27; Neff, Kirkpatrick, and Rude 2007, 140). Dina Gohar told me,

> It's the cognitive piece as well. I think of it as satisficing because that research shows some people tend to be more maximizers and some people tend to actually just settle. And I think we need to come to terms with settling, but not even feeling it is settling in a negative way. I think it's the hard part. You don't feel you've settled by giving up working 24/7—you felt it was not worth it to continue, it was no longer aligned with your values and what you wanted for your life. That doesn't get treated as a failure. A lot of it is reframing, especially because we have internalized a standard that if I'm not working, that means I'm not anything; my worth is way too dependent on productivity. The trick is not beating yourself up about it in those moments and really putting on the cognitive hat and say, "Wait a minute. My body's telling me that I need to rest. That's not a failure."

"We can't give people what we don't have," says Brené Brown (2012, 177). When you work closely with students, it can be difficult to treat them with compassion when your empathy well is dry for both them and yourself. But we can learn to be self-compassionate, to find more meaning, to move from "coping to thriving" (Nagoski and Nagoski

2019, 68). In that spirit, Katherine Segal has advice for developing a meaningful self-care plan that can help you heal from burnout.

The term "self-care" has become an overused, meaningless cliché synonymous with indulgence, numbing out, and pretending your stress isn't there. While it's not going to fit on a bumper sticker, I prefer to say, "Actions an individual can take to support their well-being" (see Segal 2020). This is not only more expansive; it gets at the purpose of what acts of self-care should be doing: supporting our well-being. Many readers may already be familiar with the dimensions of wellness model. The original model was developed in 1976 with six dimensions: social, emotional, physical, spiritual, occupational, and intellectual (Green 2016; National Wellness Institute 2019). More recent iterations of the model have included additional dimensions: mind/body, environmental, and financial (Segal 2020).

Burnout, while generally presumed to originate in the occupational wellness dimension, has the potential to negatively impact functioning in all wellness dimensions. Imagine a person broke their arm at work. While the injury occurred on the job, the arm does not spontaneously heal when it is time to clock out for the night and go home. Without proper intervention, the arm remains broken and the person not only experiences a decline in their ability to fully perform work duties but may also have difficulties away from work, such as in their ability to care for themselves. This could lead to decline in emotional well-being and then decline in interpersonal relationships as the person becomes increasingly distressed. Similarly, the impact of burnout spreads across the wellness dimensions, negatively impacting our ability to perform job functions efficiently, fully care for ourselves, and interact with the world in a meaningful manner.

When we understand burnout from this perspective, it becomes easy to see why the occasional bubble bath and shopping spree will never cure burnout. Before and during burnout it is important to identify and engage in activities that will foster healing and raise your level of satisfaction in each of the wellness dimensions.

The following activity shows how to identify the wellness dimensions most in need of your attention. To create your healing self-care plan,

1. Begin by listing the wellness dimensions on a sheet of paper.
2. Reflect on your level of satisfaction in each wellness dimension. Place a score of 0–10 next to each wellness dimension, where 0 is the least satisfaction and 10 is the most satisfaction you can feel in that category.
3. Identify which areas are in distress (scores below 5), which areas feel "okay" and need some improvement (scores 5–7), and which areas are doing well and need maintenance (scores 8–10).
4. For each wellness dimension, identify activities you can engage in to raise your level of satisfaction. For example, if your satisfaction in your physical well-being is low, identify the key issue and potential solutions. Do you need to get more sleep on a consistent basis, go to the doctor to address illnesses, or improve your eating habits?
5. Identify where on your list of potential solutions you would like to start.

As you create your healing self-care plan, tailor it to your personal needs, goals, and preferences. When possible, select action steps that interest you. For example, when creating a plan to improve your satisfaction in your physical health dimension, if the thought of jogging thirty minutes a day makes you want to fake a heart attack, pick something else that supports physical health. You may also find yourself needing to engage in action steps that are "good for you" rather than fun. For example, it may be important to go to the doctor to support your physical health or go to therapy to support your emotional health. These steps may not be fun or easy, but deep healing rather than quick fixes will result in greater benefits, sustainability, and life balance.

People with self-compassion ask for what they need but maintain boundaries and "know that growing any psychological resource, including compassion, is to have repeated experiences of it that are turned into lasting changes in neural structure or functioning" (Hanson and Hanson 2018, 15). Self-compassion can be hard in an environment like higher education, but we are all capable of fostering it, actively using it during the challenging times, and building it up as a muscle.

Conclusion

Compassion can look like many things: showing empathy and pointing others who are suffering to available resources; setting solid boundaries around when you will and will not check email; making yourself vulnerable by discussing your burnout and struggles or really listening to someone sharing these feelings with you. As women, our evolutionary tendency to "tend and befriend" predisposes many of us to caring deeply about the people we work with and care for, students included, but it can also lead us into burnout in ways men may not experience.

Perhaps because of these evolutionary and social behaviors, women may be uniquely positioned to both experience burnout and help others work through it. While it was unintentional at the time, I turned to other women initially to cope with my burnout.

What are some ways to cope with exhaustion and those depressed levels of compassion toward yourself and others? Healthy strategies are things you might expect or that might seem trivial at first: actively resting and making time for play, committing to coaching or therapy, deepening personal relationships outside work, taking meaningful breaks, practicing mindfulness, exercising and physically moving regularly, and eating and sleeping well. You might also investigate other ways to mitigate stress and to identify gaslighting so you can resist both.

I learned to offer myself grace and self-compassion, but it took a while, just as it had taken a while for my burnout to reach the level of breakdown. Once I was able to shift my mind-set away from needing external validation to understanding myself and my authentic needs, I was able to understand Katie Linder when she said, "It's important for me to have that openness to growth, asking, 'what am I supposed to be learning through the situation?' even if it's really hard or it's not ideal or even great."

Reflection Opportunity

- How can you offer yourself and those around you compassion?
- How might expressing vulnerability open up new avenues of support?
- How do we change the culture of higher ed to allow vulnerability, normalize asking for help and offering support, and shift unrealistic expectations that lead to burnout?

CHAPTER 5

Connection

As you might imagine, those moments I was unintentionally vulnerable with my colleague before the 2018 fall semester both liberated and scarred me as someone dependent on her work for identity, worth, and community. You'll remember that I told my first boss, Bob, that I was quitting because I was going back to graduate school. It was a lie at the time but also the logical next step for me to prove I belonged somewhere professionally. Higher ed made sense to me because the steps to success were so clearly laid out:* get degree, get tenure-track job, publish, teach good classes if you have to, do some leadership, get promoted with tenure, etc. Higher ed was a community to which I believed I could belong and connect with people like me, not realizing at the time that every one of those hoops I had to jump through to belong involved other people judging my worth.

A lot of factors caused my burnout rock bottom,† some of them related to the absence of connection, which led to me going on medical

---

* Ha!

† Including an adorable designer puppy named Maisie, who had zero impulse control, but that's a story for another book.

leave in the spring of 2019 for mental-health reasons. As I mentioned in the previous chapter, Laura and my psychiatrist had been urging me to step back from as much as possible at work until I could get a handle on my burnout. That advice was difficult to follow because it went against all my instincts and tapped into all my insecurities about being replaceable. How could I just off-load all the work I had, much of which I had created or led, onto others?

Ultimately, it took those two mental-health professionals, a coach, and my pre-semester office breakdown to get me to talk with others on my campus about my burnout and ask for time away. I needed to almost completely disconnect from higher education to build myself back up. For the most part, every one of them was supportive and kind. When I emailed my department chair, she immediately took that rogue first-year writing course off my hands, as well as all departmental service. I went to our associate provost, to whom we reported for the design-thinking work, and shared that I was unable to continue. He was immediately supportive and told me to step back for as long as I needed. Project collaborators were next: my departmental cohort, design-thinking program colleagues and coeditors of our in-process edited collection, and the coeditors for the disciplinary journal special issue I was leading.

I did all this help-seeking in one big burst on a Friday while I had the nerve, so naturally I spent most of the following weekend having panic attack after panic attack. I had somehow managed to ask all these colleagues for help, or at least grace, despite being convinced that my doing so would cause problems for everyone in my orbit and that I was letting them down and making their jobs harder, even though *almost* everyone I talked to had been understanding and empathetic. I knew in my gut that I had just wasted every ounce of professional capital I had and completely ruined my reputation at my institution and possibly in higher education in general. I belonged nowhere now. Surely, I had ostracized myself completely. Another failure.

But unexpectedly, I found that failure, my burnout and physical and emotional withdrawal, was the thing that would connect me with people most closely and most meaningfully.

While I was on medical leave, I attended a disciplinary conference that I had long before committed to. By that point, a good eight months after the office breakdown, I was more at peace with myself and my experience and much less afraid of the question "How are you?" There were so many people at the conference with whom I had long-standing relationships that when asked, I simply said, "I'm on medical leave for burnout." No drama or wailing, just "I have burnout."

The responses were surprising. Almost everyone commiserated and either shared their own burnout experience or pointed me to someone who was experiencing burnout and could use an ear. People wanted to get lunch or a drink so we could talk more. Others stayed with me to talk when we should have been in sessions. I gave and received a lot of hugs, with no pity to be seen. I connected to people as humans, not just professional faculty or administrators or those I perceived as having control over my worth. Burnout leveled the playing field and highlighted our common cultural experience, one that was so often buried and hidden but had actually touched many of us in our isolation.

And in making those connections there was, and is, comfort and strength and change.

Reflection Opportunity

- What does connection mean to you?
- What are the three most important connections in your life right now? What is special about these connections?

- What are the three most important connections in your work? What is special about them?
- What connections would be hardest to live without?

Connection, Competition, and Outside Observers

CONNECTION

I've included connection as one of the four pillars of burnout resilience because it's (1) something I don't think I've ever been good at, (2) the thing burnout took first from me, and (3) the action that was most important to overcoming my burnout. Burnout is a cultural signal that the patriarchal nature of higher ed, with its focus on achievement, productivity, and rugged individuality, is at odds with the best interests of academic women, faculty of color, non-tenure-track and adjunct faculty, and even graduate students. If I had not connected to others, I never would have realized how common my situation was or in what good company I was in feeling this fear of disconnection from what I had always seen as my safe community in higher education.

In her book *Hivemind* (2019), Sarah Rose Cavanagh explores how the evolutionary importance of connection and belonging is at odds with the philosophy of American individualism, as well as the idea that belonging is a key to mental health. Flourishing requires belonging, community, and social support from others who "share a common understanding of how the world works and which values to uphold" (221). Like any community, academics crave to belong and be appreciated, and building community is an evolutionary imperative for our health and happiness (225), which was definitely true for me in higher ed.

Humans thrive in collaborative communities, where they feel a sense of belonging and meaningful contribution to shared goals and values. Healthy workplace cultures foster social support among community members by creating a climate of trusting relationships and amiable interactions between colleagues in the pursuit of shared goals (Esfahani Smith 2017, 49–50). Sabagh, Hall, and Saroyan (2018) found that the higher the level of social and administrative support in an academic culture, the less likely members are to report feelings of burnout (138). But that support is not necessarily or inherently created in the context of higher ed institutions.

Burnout is a social problem in workplace cultures, especially in higher education, where that sense of belonging, support, and mutual pursuits is absent or replaced by ongoing conflicts, active or under the surface. Jonathan Malesic (2016) maintains that "academic culture fosters burnout when it encourages overwork, promotes a model of professors as isolated entrepreneurs, and offers little recognition for good teaching or mentoring. The persistent financial stress on colleges and universities only exacerbates the problem."

The stresses associated with higher ed are real and pervasive. For me, burnout initially presented as depression and the heightening of my existing competitive instinct. I ramped up competition with everyone around me, which unfortunately led to conflict, conflict that I regret but that also showed me I needed another path. Departmental, institutional, or even disciplinary conflict and competition can be disenfranchising and make resilience challenging.

COMPETITION

In the academy, there seems to be no such thing as overwork. This calling, a.k.a. job, required all of me to do it well and stay competitive, which is likely why I had so many nemeses at different points in my life and career. To stay competitive at my institution, one filled with remarkable and dedicated teacher-scholar-mentors, I compared myself with everyone, especially some of my closest colleagues.

Since everyone seemed to be working just as hard as I was, if not harder, in their leadership roles and directorships, surely my relentless pace was appropriate and positioning me for similar leadership opportunities. Because I had distanced myself from everyone when the burnout came on, but also ramped up comparing myself with those around me, I didn't have a truly informed sense of why I felt so competitive with others while feeling weak and vulnerable at the same time, except that I was afraid of being forgotten or overlooked in my suffering.

I didn't know until after my breakdown and having to ask my chair and dean for a medical leave that others had been very worried about the pace at which I was forcing myself to run. Two senior colleagues in my office suite later told me they had been worried for some time, that I had always been sick and looked frustrated and exhausted all the time. And my chair would eventually tell me she had been concerned for my health every time she read my year-end self-evaluation document. I don't know if I would have listened to them if they had told me these things before burnout, but because I had distanced myself, I had robbed myself of their perspective and compassion, which might have impacted my work and life earlier.

INSIDE OUTSIDE OBSERVERS

The other person who saw my spiral was the person closest to me, my husband. My partner is not an academic, and because he did not go to a traditional four-year undergraduate institution, he has no preconceived notions of what higher ed is or the way it "behaves." A software engineer, he tends to see things more in black and white than I do, always looks for a way to fix things, has an easier time delineating between work and personal time, and is less prone to internalizing stress related to work because he has hobbies that allow him to blow off steam. He also has been with me through five years of graduate school, twelve years on the tenure track and tenured, and more, so he experienced every breakdown, every crushing meeting or failure, and every "I should be" for seventeen years.

As he tried to support me, he would regularly say many of the same things. If I was incensed by a situation with peers that was toxic, he'd ask who my boss was and why I couldn't take the situation to human resources. He'd ask why I let certain people talk to me the way they did, and I didn't have many answers except not wanting to piss off someone up the chain. When I was exhausted or sick, he'd argue for me to stay home and take care of myself rather than go to class or a meeting (I almost always went anyway). And countless times he'd tell me that I couldn't continue to take it all on myself and stay healthy for us and our future. He was right, of course.

My husband* wasn't the only partner sounding alarms about the toxic nature of the work and culture of higher ed and how it impacted academics' well-being. For many women with whom I spoke, those closest to them playing the same role. Kelly J. Baker told me that her partner also played a key role in helping her understand her relationship to her work:

> In my last academic job as a lecturer, I did a three-hour seminar to get all my classes in and, supposedly, work on my own stuff in my free time. It took thirty-five minutes to get home, so I would call my partner and say, "Once again, it's your job to tell me why I'm not going to quit my job tomorrow. Right? This is what you're going to have to do: you're going to have to walk me through the things I like about this work, because I hate all of it right now." I hated doing scholarship. I hated dealing with people in the department. I did still like students; students were the good

---

* While the couples mentioned in this section are all in heterosexual marriages, this is another instance of not having more diversity to draw from due to who responded to my requests for interviews or the available research.

part for me. But I was at a place where everything about this job sucked—everything. He had to talk me through that every week not because he wanted me to stay somewhere I was so unhappy but because he knew I'd need to finish out the semester to feel good about it.

And when I decided to quit and go freelance, he supported me. At one point, though, I came to him and said, "I just don't think I produce enough." And he had this moment where you could see the record scratch, you know, like "Did she really just say that?" He couldn't even wrap his head around the fact that I could even think that. As if it would be possible for me to think that with all the stuff I had done, somehow I was still not productive in some sort of way. Seeing it through his eyes, this mentality, of course, sets you up again for your work to burn you out and for you to hate it.

Elizabeth also acknowledges her partner for calling her out on the occasions when her work become an overwhelming feature in her and her family's well-being:

I credit my husband as the person who could help me see in from the outside of higher ed, who made me see that my academic life wasn't sustainable. My family paid a lot of a price. You know, I was on that tenure wheel with a baby. But one of those conversations that sparked things was my husband saying, You have to decide who you love more: academia and your students or your family. He said, I'm going to ask you to make a choice because one way or another we can't live this way. You can live in some degree of balance, how we define it, but you can't be doing what they want you to do because you have nothing left for us. It sounds harsh maybe to hear that from the outside, but he was the only person watching me do everything. He saw they were still telling me to jump higher, and he came from a place of love.

But it wasn't easy. Until last year, I worked over every family vacation. Like, what is vacation? You don't work during vacation? I stayed up until one o'clock; I was sometimes not awake in the morning because I had been up until two working on something. I didn't realize how much of a leap that was going to be cognitively and emotionally because I kept trying to sneak off and do work stuff. And he kept busting me. I didn't know what to do otherwise. My husband told me I was going to have to unlearn a lot of habits in order to be able to relax and own my time with my family as sacred. I needed his perspective to see how higher ed had taken over my life.

One woman with whom I spoke realized how much conflict with her peers over job duties and grant money were affecting her homelife when her 5-year-old daughter asked her why she was angry all the time. Yet another's partner said they liked summer best because they "got her back." These aren't isolated stories. We'll discuss this more in the next chapter, on balance, but here I want to articulate three places to find connection in a culture of burnout: inside the institution, outside the institution, and outside the academy.

Reflection Opportunity

- What are some connections in your life that you have energy for? Where does that energy come from?
- What are you tolerating in your life in terms of connection? What are you putting up with that maybe you haven't even thought about changing?
- Who or what might you connect with to help build burnout resilience?
- What actions can you take to bring more connection into your life?
- What connections does fear keep you from making?

Inside the Institution

One primary place we look for connection is our institutions. In these sites of immediate community faculty can "share praise, comfort, happiness, and humor with people they like and respect," as well as assistance and other forms of support (Maslach, Schaufeli, and Leiter 2001, 415). In a study of faculty developers, Klodiana Kolomitro, Natasha Kenny, and Suzanne Le-May Sheffield (2020) found that "colleagues who were supportive, empathetic, respectful, caring, competent, appreciative, helpful, and enthusiastic had a positive impact" (4). Having colleagues who are supportive and also receive support is crucial to connection and community and therefore to warding off burnout. For much of my time at my previous institution, I had those colleagues in a variety of different groups I belonged to before I began isolating myself, but relationships change over time, and old arguments take on new life.

As Maslach, Schaufeli, and Leiter (2001) argue, "Some jobs isolate people from each other or make social contact impersonal. However, what is most destructive is chronic and unresolved conflict with others on the job. Such conflict produces constant negative feelings of frustration and hostility and reduces the likelihood of social support" (415). Kolomitro, Kenny, and Le-May Sheffield (2020) list a variety of challenges to connection as well, including professional jealousy, coasting and loafing, gossiping, passive-aggressive behavior, lack of clarity and transparency, and general hostility (5).

Aarohi's story illustrates some of the challenges of not having social support in your environment:

> As Aarohi was wrapping up her PhD work, she was thrilled to hear that she had been offered a tenure-track appointment co-leading the lab of a researcher she had idolized as a grad student. He would be retiring

soon and needed someone to move the lab forward. While interviewing for the position, she had met the PI and the postdoc fellows she'd be working with most closely. This was a career-making opportunity, and she couldn't wait to get started. The last few years as a student from India during such divisive immigration policies was very difficult, but this new experience would be worth it.

To start, before she developed her own research arm in the lab, Aarohi most looked forward to reviewing and writing up the extensive data the lab had collected in multiple longitudinal studies through the lens of her own specialty. She first realized something was not right in the lab when she saw the state of the data. And the more she worked to understand it, the more she also realized that the postdocs she thought she would be directing turned out to be, well, unprofessional.

When she shared her concerns with the PI, a white man ten years past retirement age, he would listen but not do anything other than offer encouragement and platitudes. He was right in the sense that as the tenure-track person she needed to manage the postdocs, but they were not researchers she had brought in, and they seemed to resent working for her and not the original PI.

Disillusioned, Aarohi was burning out in the lab environment. She saw shoddy work around her, but the lab was also bringing in millions of dollars in funding seemingly on the name of her PI alone. Her postdocs were lazy and generally made things difficult and unpleasant. She began to doubt herself: if everyone around her thought this was what good work looked like, what was wrong with her that she couldn't see that? Were her expectations too high? Why couldn't she just suck it up, analyze the bad data, and write it up? She found herself retreating from the lab and the people in it, but working long hours to write up the existing data was not the scientist and supervisor she wanted to be.

We'll return to Aarohi's story in the next section. Unlike Aarohi, several women I spoke with, especially women of color, shared how having a group of women inside their institutions allowed them to receive support but also offer it as well. Jennifer Snodgrass found that spending time with her junior colleagues was enriching for her, writing:

> Someone asked me the other day how I kept such a positive disposition. I simply replied, "I spend as much time as I can with the junior faculty." They laughed as if I was being sarcastic, to which I replied I was serious. I have found that spending time with my younger colleagues has encouraged me to think outside the box, to be more creative, to take risks, and not to take myself too seriously. It has been in these relationships with my junior faculty that I have found honesty and an absence of egos. I find their outlook to be refreshing and one that helps me to reevaluate my own purposes, even as a full professor. If this is not in your current practice, I encourage you to invite a junior faculty member out to a meal. Both parties will benefit from this dialogue.

Like Snodgrass, Cassandra and Andrea found strength in numbers. "When I accepted a tenure-track offer at a small institution," said Cassandra,

> I knew absolutely nothing about the semirural community we were moving to. I was calling HR with a ton of questions, including, Are there other Black people I can talk to in this community? Where do I go to get my hair done? Are there people who can tell me where it's safe for my family to live in town? Will my Black children have trouble at school? I needed these basic questions answered. HR did hook me up with a woman in my department, and she introduced me to a group of

women of color, who have been lifesavers, even before we got to campus. We meet regularly in small or larger groups, we go to campus events together, and our kids play together. My closest relationships in this place are with those women.

And Andrea stated,

I'm in an NTT year-to-year research position, and I teach one course per semester. There were several of us hired at the same time, and no one in the department really pays much attention to us, maybe because of our contingent role or, more troubling, because we are all women of color, but we have one another as role models and confidantes. Every year, those of us in my position are told there might not be money to extend our contracts. Some of us have been fired and rehired before an academic year even ends. It's hard not to isolate yourself from others in your same role because we are basically fighting for the same funding, but we know we are stronger together, even if we are just there to vent and share our outrage with one another. We always keep one another informed of things happening in the department. We give one another emotional and practical support.

As in Andrea's story, contingent faculty are often deeply affected by a lack of connection in their roles. In conversations with fellow non-tenure-track faculty, Bridget Lepore explored the idea of and desire for community for faculty in contingent roles, finding that connection and relationships were crucial to avoiding or beating burnout:

In trying to manage their feelings of being overwhelmed, anxiety, and burnout, many of the faculty I spoke to were likely to search for connection to their colleagues and the institutions as a whole.

Connection seemed to be a way of managing how they responded to their working conditions. One faculty member who had left her position spoke of the value of these colleagues, saying that even though she had left the university, she still had these connections to draw strength from. She remarked, "I have a core group I will always be connected to. I think when you are working under difficult conditions, it encourages bonding, because you are working under circumstances that are not ideal, and no one can understand that unless they are with you."

This comment and many of the stories I heard from NTTs reiterates the idea that non-tenure-track faculty build relationships and professional connections in the same way that tenured faculty do. Challenging conditions may make connection critical for contingent faculty, since they often do not have access to the professional networking resources that are available to tenured and tenure-track faculty.

While preventing burnout takes a great deal of work at the organizational level, the faculty I spoke with had suggestions for how individuals can take steps toward a healthier career life. While changes can be made at the institutional and the departmental or program level, they may not be helpful for individual faculty who are struggling right now. For those struggling right now, the advice of those who have been there is to connect and to focus on connection—to colleagues, to students, and to the mission that you believe in.

Connection is a key factor in surviving burnout. When we are tired and overwhelmed, it seems like a good idea to retreat from work and avoid others. For the faculty I spoke with, connecting, which it often took time and care to make happen, was important.

Even things as simple as brief scheduled coffee meetings with colleagues can affect burnout levels. Working and talking with colleagues can be energizing and motivational, as shared experiences create a bond and allow faculty to release stress and gain clarity on situations that they are dealing with.

Among the many ideas that show promise for professional learning that can also address some of the conditions of burnout are models that allow NTT faculty to learn on an ongoing basis with their peers: communities of practice, faculty learning communities, critical friends' groups, and reading circles. While these models require different levels of planning and support, they all focus on enhancing teaching and learning, contributing to ongoing efforts, and encouraging social learning. Each can be tailored to the faculty group and its mission, allowing deep and meaningful connection and learning.

Recovering from burnout is a process that takes time and intent. Since burnout is not just related to systemic or environmental factors but is linked to identity and history as well, it makes sense that leaving the situation is not enough to undo it. Personally, I found that it took time to build a different professional life—one where my work was the same but the way I approached it was different. The factors that contribute to burnout remain the same, and for most overworked NTT faculty they are unavoidable. I found, though, that mind-set changes along with changes in work habits, more writing, and involvement in professional groups helped me reclaim my professionalism and move forward with more energy.

Connecting professionally with people at your own institution can be very valuable but is not always easy. Connecting with other academics at other institutions can also provide the validation, support, and collegiality needed to stave off or mitigate burnout.

Outside the Institution

In the words of Angela Lumpkin (2014), "Rich are the faculty members who count among their strongest allies colleagues committed to helping them grow and develop throughout their careers" (203).

One of the most common themes that arose in my research and interviews with women academics was the importance of a support group or back channel for both connection and compassion. Women more than men define ourselves in our relationships to and with others in connected knowing (Nagoski and Nagoski 2019). Providing and receiving social support is critical to processing our knowledge and experiences and managing our well-being. In a study on imposter syndrome in academics, for example, Hutchins and Rainbolt (2017) found that women, much more so than men, actively sought social support in the form of listening, offering advice, empathizing, and resourcing when facing imposter thoughts (206).

Sometimes, the best social support comes from outside one's institution, because those offering it are free of the history, politics, and emotions of that institution. I have had a Facebook Messenger group chat with graduate-school peers at my own and other institutions since 2010. It started as a way to communicate about a shared interest at a disciplinary conference, and over the years it morphed into a tight-knit circle of friends who are there as anything from collaborators to commiserators, from a "no committee" to cheerleaders. For the January 23, 2021, episode of my podcast *the agile academic*, I spoke with the women faculty friends in the group about the value of these relationships, and they provided some important insights into how this kind of connection has impacted them and their lives:

RPR: And I think for us, at least for me, the connection piece has fed all of the other things. I think we started out as collegial friends. We started out as supporting each other. It's turned into developing projects together and so many other things. I'm just curious what each of your perspectives is on our back channel. We have a Facebook chat that we've had for ten years. I would love to download the records on that. Can you imagine? It would be like eight feet tall? How is it useful to you, or how does it fit into your professional life?

ASHLEY PATRIARCA: You all are the place where I run when I have questions, and I often have a lot of questions because going through the tenure process or even when I was on the job market, y'all were telling me to calm down, and everything was going to be okay. I didn't believe you in both situations. And then it was fine. I know that's not the case all the time, but it was really important for me to have that sort of reassurance that other folks had gone through the process and had survived and made it through. And that even if it didn't feel like it was going to work out at that point, for me, it did. And it was so helpful—that mentorship, that guidance, that reassurance.

SANDY FRENCH: I'm thinking specifically of connections and balance. I think it's very cool that we're all close in age, but we're not all the same age. We're close in where we are in our careers, but not exactly the same place in our careers. And so every time someone has a question, there's a balanced perspective that comes from being close to people who are not in your institution. There's an objectivity in the sounding board that you may not get from the connections you have at your own institution, which are also important. But it's that balanced perspective, where we're just as likely to cheer each other on as we are to say, you know, maybe your dean has a point, or maybe that student had something else going on. It's a safe place where people can kind of tell you to check yourself, but it's not the end of a relationship. It doesn't mean you're a terrible professor. I think there's something really beautiful about being able to talk to people who aren't at your institution.

JENNIFER VELTSOS: As usual, Sandy says everything I'm thinking, but so much better. That's how I was thinking to describe you all. I imagine a continuum, and on one end it's cheerleading. And on the other end I have a "no committee." You are also my no committee. If I'm not sure about something and I need some other perspectives that I can trust or I need to be vulnerable, I can do that with you all. And then there's everything in between. There's no judgment. It really helps. And I probably have not mentioned this particular benefit to you all, but in this past year, as an administrator, I really have to self-censor. So you all have helped me when I need to vent. Sometimes you're the only ones that I can talk to about things because you're completely removed from the situation. So, thank you for that.

RPR: You were there with me when I was going through the burnout and pre-burnout, not knowing what was happening to me. During that time, I got some misdiagnoses along the way, and we talked through those to see what I could reasonably do: Was it okay if I decide to leave my institution, even though I'd been there for so long and assumed that I was going to retire there? There are also a couple male colleagues in our back channel, so we also have the sub–back channel just for us. There are some things that are only appropriate for the ladies, at least at first, and we've done that too with sexism that has come up and where we needed just the four of us to share that perspective.

I think these back channels are just so important, especially for women in higher education. Having that voice in the background to hold you up no matter what happens, but also, like SF said, check us if we need to be checked, but we know how to do it in a way that's calming almost. I can vent, but you're not going to throw it in my face. You're going to share experiences, or you're going to commiserate. And then you're either going to offer me some wonderful advice, or you're going to tell me that I need to step back and rethink something.

Our experience connecting regularly with a specific group of people isn't uncommon. Several of the women I spoke with also mentioned the importance of a back channel with friends and colleagues beyond their institutions where they could be themselves, ask potentially embarrassing professional questions, and just generally be there for one another. Jennifer Snodgrass writes that she found support in a collective of women from different universities:

There are times where those of us in academia need to vent about a student or colleague, a new policy or procedure, or even the latest trends in our field. Many times, these vent sessions do not need to occur with colleagues on your campus, as they may just be too close to the situation. And they certainly do *not* need to occur on any social media platform. I have found great solace and honest friendship in a group of women outside my university. We established a protected online group site where we can post our successes and discuss our concerns. These friendships are my go-to when I see even the slightest signs of burnout. I am accountable to them, and they are to me. I also seek out friendships that bring out my inner joy, and the minute I find myself in self-doubt, I send a quick text or message for a bit of reality. These friendships take time, so seek out opportunities when possible to form those types of connections.

Helen benefits from two different groups of women for support in different areas of her life:

> I have two back-channel groups I draw support from. One is with friends from college, and we talk more about mom stuff than work. And I have another group with three friends from graduate school. As women in a technical field, we use our chat to offer partnership validation, encouragement, and a space to vent. This group is a lifeline for me; we often text multiple times a day, and I know I can share anything with them, from failures and frustrations to wins and celebrations. They are my go-to people, and I'm grateful to have them in my life.

For each of the women in groups like these, there was a safe space where they could be vulnerable and open in ways that were not possible with institutional colleagues, regardless of how strong those relationships might be. Institutional colleagues don't have the emotional and psychological distance from situations, nor are they removed from the structures of power that could impact the way we talk about our challenges. Returning to Aarohi's story, she found some of the support she needed outside of her lab:

> With this doubt and disenchanted, wondering if her PhD was even worth it, Aarohi went to a conference where she introduced herself to a more senior woman she respected and knew did good work in her specialty. This researcher had seen some of her publications and was

interested in discussing how that intersected with the work in her own lab. After talking at the conference and several more times after that, they struck up a collaboration that excited Aarohi, one that really let her unique specialty shine.

Along the way, her new mentor helped her think through what was happening in her lab and what her options were in terms of working with the postdocs and PI and helped her define a path in her role that made sense, especially when she would be the lab's PI and go up for tenure and promotion eventually. This outside perspective validated that unfortunately what she was experiencing was common but also gave her ideas about how to deal with her PI and postdocs until she moved into the PI role. Connecting with this new mentor reinvigorated Aarohi, and she's looking forward to their continued collaboration and her next career steps.

Outside perspectives were valuable, and necessary, for each of these women to thrive in their faculty roles and to, if not prevent, then at least ward off some of the symptoms of burnout that come along with stressful work and unclear expectations. Having those connections outside their institutions provided necessary perspective on their careers in both the present and the future.

Sharon Mitchler encourages women faculty to build an academic support network with people beyond your own campus, writing:

> Holy cats and kittens, but there is so much drama that can develop from working with a relatively small group of people on your own campus, perhaps a bit too closely and a bit too intensely. I struggle to remain even remotely objective once my emotional hackles are up, or when a meeting has become a little testy. That emotional drain may sap your energy fast, so having peers at other institutions who can give you more thoughtful feedback, listen to your concerns, let you vent a bit in

safety, or ask you a question that you are more willing to consider outside your own academic context are invaluable.

Look for these people across social media platforms, local or regional conferences, or in multi-institutional research groups. The people who were in graduate school with you are often working for other institutions, so they are another good source for off-campus support.

And in addition to important perspectives from colleagues and friends both within one's institution and then within higher ed more broadly, women faculty members also need people we can trust outside higher ed altogether.

Outside Higher Ed

As I shared earlier in this chapter, those close to us often see the warning signs of burnout long before we do, and connecting with people and activities completely outside academia can be important for finding a more balanced, connected you. Padilla and Thompson (2016) found quite simply that "more social support, hours spent with family, hours spent on leisure activities, [and] hours spent sleeping are related to a decrease in burnout among faculty" (554). Writing from her experience, Sharon Mitchler shares,

> Our work will subsume whatever else is around it, just like a black hole pulling in stars. Expect that because there is always more work to do, and because we are responsible for getting our own work done, we will not always exercise the best time-management judgment. However, when you have people and activities away from the job, it is healthier. Those emotional bonds, those other experiences, are necessary for you to be a person, not just an academic machine.

I need to spend time with people who don't care about the details of my work in order to "snap off" my constant listing of tasks. Oh, yeah. I'm a crazy list maker, even when the list cannot be completed. So I make specific time to be around people who couldn't care less about my work and care a lot about me. I hike, I tap dance (oh, so very badly) with great enthusiasm because that keeps me from being hyper-attached to my profession. The people whom I share these interests with don't want to hear about my work. They expect me to focus on hiking or tap dancing or whatever is interesting in that community.

Sarah and Caitlin also exemplify how women found connection outside of the academy. "In our twenties," said Sarah,

my best friend and I saw an article in *Real Simple* magazine about women's weekend retreats and decided to give it a try. That was twenty years ago. Twice a year, once in the summer and once in the fall, our group of friends and family members gathers somewhere fun to reset, work through problems and challenges, talk about our lives and work and families and dreams, do fun activities. Whenever I'm going through something, I'll often think, "Oh, I can take that to Womyn's Weekend," because I know that's a supportive community who knows me well and can help me through whatever it is, just as I will for them. (Cavanagh 2021)

And Caitlin recalled,

When I started running, I didn't really think of myself as someone who exercises, but I started running and that became part of my identity. To get stronger for running, I decided to try Crossfit. People had warned me, including the trainer at the gym, that is was really hard and intense, but that made me want to do it more. I saw immediately that this group was a family. There is no hiding from one another physically but also emotionally because emotions come to the surface when you push your body in this way. We see one another experiencing emotions and love one another for it. There is no judgment; we understand we are all at different points in our fitness journeys, but we are in it together for support and encouragement. (Faas 2021)

As I discuss in more detail in the next chapter, I found connection in an unexpected place—a barn. During my first sabbatical, in 2013, I finally caved to my husband's constant nagging that I needed a hobby. I started taking horseback-riding lessons and leased a horse to ride whenever I wanted. After a year at the barn where I learned all the

---

EASY, EXCITING, AND EXTREME

Having thought deeply about connection and what you want to bring into your life as a means to prevent or address burnout, what are some direct actions you can take now to build connection and support your burnout resilience? The table below asks you to think about three categories of possibilities: the easy things you could do today, the steps you could take that would require more effort but are still exciting to think about, and finally the wacky, out-there, bold ways you might add connection to your life. Once you have finished your brainstorm, pick one thing in each column to pursue this month. Journaling about your adventures can capture the connections and growth you experience while reaching out.

Easy	Exciting	Extreme

---

basics, I moved to a different barn, a more professional space where I could take lessons in dressage specifically. At this farm, Highclere, I found three kindred spirits—two human and one equine. These connections allowed me to explore a different side of what made me happy, completely outside higher education.

I spoke to other women faculty who reported finding communities outside higher ed to be crucial. Alumni groups offered venues to engage with people who shared a common experience. Women told me about attending alum events, serving on their undergraduate institutions' boards, and also tapping into networks associated with Greek letter or honorary organizations. I, for example, volunteered for my national social sorority, serving as an adviser to campus undergraduate women and doing other service work. Doing so connected me to a large network of women with at least one shared point of commonality; years after concluding my service I am still close to some of them. Others reported finding satisfaction working with service and philanthropic organizations, as community event planners, or with parent groups.

Connecting to nature, exercising one's creativity, and pursuing a hobby were also mentioned as ways to connect not only with others but also with oneself and the world around one. We'll explore these avenues for connection in the next chapter.

Connection was one of the first things burnout robbed me of. But then bonding with other faculty experiencing burnout helped me discover that I wasn't alone in my experience and that it wasn't my fault. While I might be publicly vocal about my burnout period, many other academic women experiencing burnout aren't ready to identify it, much less talk about it openly with others. As I've said before, our task is to normalize talking about burnout without normalizing the culture that causes it. If we work to remove the strain and stigma attached to burnout, we can forge the connections crucial to our own healing and to changing the culture.

CHAPTER 6

Balance

As I write this, I'm sitting on a wide veranda on a hot summer day in rural Georgia, watching a large herd of horses of all shapes and sizes graze around me. I've spent hours on trails and walks through the ranging pasture in the last few days on the back of a large blue roan gelding named Billy. I didn't think much as Billy and I ambled. We just observed the scenery—other horses, deer, fox squirrels, and birds chittering at us, telling us not to step on their ground nests. I had a stray thought every once in a while that I should bend the walk-only rules and break Billy into a good run to see what he could do. But the urges passed, and I was peaceful again. We watched from afar as some randy colts raced down the field stretching their legs and trying to impress the fillies. Later, I set Billy to graze for a few hours until we would venture out on the trails again.

A horse pasture with a stocked barn is one of the only places where I don't think about work. I'm a committed indoorsy introvert unless horses are involved. When I was growing up, horses were reserved for camp and vacation, but I started riding in earnest in 2014, while I was on sabbatical writing my first book. As I've mentioned, my husband is an avid hobbyist and had been on me for years to "find a hobby" as totally engrossing as his are. I needed something that would take over my mind and push work into the recesses, he claimed.

When I started riding, I was taking group lessons with 10-year-olds from an instructor who didn't know what to make of me. I was good with that because I could just focus on listening to and taking care of my equine partner. Horses are like dogs in a way; they have a keen sense of their human partner's mood and tend to mirror it back to you. So, if you are happy, enjoying a walk with them, they are happy too.* But if you are tense or frustrated, they will mirror that back to you in orneriness and sass. In any case, the horse is trying to teach you to listen to yourself and to him, to fully focus in those moments together.

I rode and took dressage lessons for a few years through the oncoming burnout, just enjoying the change of pace. If you're wondering, dressage is to show jumping what ice dancing is to ice skating at the Olympics. It's all groundwork and control rather than showy jumps and speed. The best rider-horse pairs look like they are dancing in the ring. It's beautiful and peaceful to watch, incredibly hard to do.

But when the burnout set in, it became harder to drag myself to the barn, to connect with my leased horse, Cody, whom I used to love just grooming and giving seemingly innumerable carrots from my magical pocket. The more the burnout got into my head, the more our relationship eroded. I was always frustrated in the ring, and he would walk me into walls to try to put me in my place. My self-talk turned inward and dark, arguing that I was a terrible rider who couldn't even keep up with the little kids learning to ride in the baby ring, that Cody hated me, that there was no way I could ever compete so why was I even doing this at all, and my favorite, that I should be writing.

* Usually. Horses can sometimes be in a bad mood too.

So I stopped riding. It was clearly a waste of my time. I made excuses to my friend who owned the barn. I stopped my lease on Cody because it was a waste of money. I ignored or snapped at my husband when he asked when I had last been to the barn. There was no point. Riding was just one more thing on my long to-do list rather than the engrossing escape it had been when I started.

So how did I end up on that veranda, months after my lowest point, watching the colts play and the mares tend their foals? I eventually (but still not completely) stopped letting the burnout tell me what I could and could not do. And I retaught myself, or maybe taught myself for the first time, that a life that's just work isn't much of a life. I needed balance. I just needed to figure out what that was.

But before we dig into this chapter, I want to say that this has been hard to write. We can talk about rest, silencing all the shoulds, or finding work-life balance, or integration, or whatever the latest term is, but the long and short of it is that balance is privilege. As I write about riding horses, resisting the culture of busyness, and having a hobby, I write as a middle-class straight white woman with no children in a two-income household. I fully acknowledge how challenging or even alien these things might be for women in different familial, cultural, and workplace situations. Representing these voices has been especially difficult in this chapter. As I discussed in the introduction, there are missing voices throughout—women who likely have more on their plates or are dealing with intersecting systems of oppression and didn't have the time, energy, or desire to share their stories. I want to honor those women here.

Reflection Opportunity

- What stories do you tell yourself about balance?
- What do you do when you aren't "doing" higher ed?

- What would balance look like in an ideal world?
- What is most challenging for you when you think about balance?

Caught in the Cycle

I had no idea how to relax before burnout and even well into my treatment. My idea of relaxing was never more than a massage or a pedicure, maybe a day off to go shopping or to drive three hours to the beach. Sustaining more than that was unthinkable. For my fortieth birthday, we went to Jamaica, where I took riding lessons every day and spent the afternoons on the beach . . . reading books about pedagogy and design thinking for work.

Work was essentially my whole life. During my years as a faculty member, my family was five hundred miles away; most of my friends had kids, who were always doing swim club or cheerleading or something; and my only really close relationship was with my husband. This was owing in part to social anxiety, which caused me to skip out on a lot of parties, to the point where I was no longer invited. But it was also because I didn't know how to turn my brain off. I was always writing an article in my head or working out a teaching problem or worrying about the sorority chapter I mentored. Work was pretty much all I thought about. But I also wondered constantly if anyone was noticing what I was doing, how I could make people notice me.* If I worked harder and achieved more, maybe people would finally care.

The coach and psychology professor Kristina Hallett (2018) says that many of her clients often feels this ways as well, as they are "caught in the cycle of high performance leading to higher performance, without

---

* Often I didn't say hello to people I knew at conferences because I didn't think they would remember me and that would just be awkward and embarrassing for me. Better to look aloof and snobbish, I guess?

maintaining balance" (115). She says that this often causes guilt, feelings of not being good enough, and the roller coaster of "I should, but I can't" and "I need to, but I don't want to" (115).

Academia breeds the belief that we must always be working and producing to be worthy and recognized. That's exhausting. But then we don't know how to relax and rest, so it's a vicious cycle.

Balancing Imbalances

When I collected stories for this book, not very many people besides the coaches who work with faculty spoke of balance. Some women did talk about imbalance though, as we have seen in previous chapters. For several of the women I spoke with, work and life were often in conflict rather than in balance or alignment. Grant deadlines conflicted with family time, grading and course prep with time out with friends, committee-meeting battles (or boredom) with helping kids do their homework. All of this was also compounded significantly during the COVID-19 pandemic, especially for women caring for young children or older family members.

For many faculty, work is always in the back of our minds even when we try to relax and enjoy being present. Celeste Headlee (2020) contends that "we've lost the balance between striving to improve and feeling gratitude for what we have. We've lost touch with the things that really enrich our lives and make us feel content" (xvii). From the perspective of academic capitalism, I think one reason, aside from the unrelenting guilt we feel when we are not working, is that we were never taught to be *content* with our work; therefore, any "leisure" time is time wasted. Summarizing research on faculty time, Timothy Thomason (2012) states, rightly, that "there is no easy metric to determine when 'enough' work has been done" for faculty who find themselves spread too thin, pulled by teaching, research, service, and all the emotional labor hiding under the surface, especially the extra emotional labor women and faculty of color do (30). The thoughts "I should" and "I need to" creep in until we can't enjoy the rest or personal time because we are always thinking about work. And when we can't judge when enough work is enough, don't know how to experience leisure, and are never content, we fall into workaholism (Hallett 2018, 86), which impacts and is impacted by our physical health and self-care.

Of course, workaholism isn't always a personality trait; it is often a very real necessity. The COVID-19 pandemic, for example, magnified many of the challenges and biases affecting working mothers, especially those with children under 5, single and BIPOC mothers, and those in precarious faculty positions. Multiple studies pulled together during 2020 showed the negative impact on productivity in terms of number of articles submitted and grant funding applied for among women academics, especially mothers (see, e.g., Krukowski, Jagsi, and Cardel 2021). Jessica Malisch and colleagues (2020) argue that some women also deal with more stressful financial challenges in their precarity (15379).

Regardless of one's relationship to the pandemic, creating a sense of balance in higher ed is difficult, to say the very least, and what will come of these pandemic stressors and inequities only time will tell. Kryss Shane has some words of encouragement for contingent faculty trying to balance the imbalances and still be mindful of their own well-being.

Dear Potentially Burned-Out Badass,

First of all, don't you roll your eyes at me. I get it; you don't feel like a Badass. But you are. You are someone who responds to the needs of many. You hear your students' anxieties, you listen to your colleagues' complaints, you write and rewrite syllabi, you juggle your own needs against the realities of the miniscule paycheck adjuncts get paid, you attend unnecessary meeting after unnecessary meeting, you show up and you show up and you show up. You're exhausted. And you're a Badass.

It's okay that you sometimes fill your stomach with takeout because you're too tired to cook. It's okay that you sometimes fill your brain with reality TV because you're too tired to think. It's okay that you prefer the company of your pet or your plant rather than that of people at networking events. It isn't all fun and games to work from home when what you really want is an office and a tenure-track job.

I know it isn't easy to cobble together your income from three different universities, all of whom say they love you while offering you adjunct role after adjunct role, never seeming to recognize that you've worked so hard that they ought to be giving you a job with benefits. You may have non-academic work that feels like settling but is necessary to pay all of the bills. You may not have nearly enough in retirement, or you think it's laughable to think about saving for retirement on top of trying to pay down student loans and/or medical debt from working yourself into illness. You read the articles about adjuncts who live in their cars or part-time staff who literally work themselves to death. I know you worry because you relate so much to those people. They too were Badasses.

I also know that you don't get apologized to nearly enough. On behalf of those who should have said this . . . I apologize for the times you have been blamed or reprimanded or fired because an entitled student complained when you graded them accurately and they received a grade that wasn't what they wanted. For piling more work onto your plate that you don't get paid for because I've been in my tenured position for so long that I forgot not everyone is in the same position. For mandatory office meetings that could have just been an email. For the crummy pay.

I apologize for the times you wonder whether anyone will ever fully utilize you for the degrees you earned. For the anxiety you feel while you wait to hear whether your contract will be renewed for the following term or quarter or semester or academic year. For the tooth pain or the squinting or the muscle aches you feel that you haven't addressed with a medical professional because you don't have health insurance through your job. For the stress and the anxiety and the depression you may struggle with because you are not feeling seen or heard or wanted or appreciated for the Badass you are.

It's okay that you don't always remember that you're a Badass. I know that you have so, so much on your plate and on your mind. I also know that the only way to survive and thrive in academia is to ask for, offer, and accept the support of others, whether in person or via social media connections. So, I encourage you to reach out. I encourage you to speak up. I encourage you to let others love on you when you need it and to offer your support when others are in need. Because the only way to validate our individual and collective Badassness is to do it together ... otherwise, it can't be considered peer-reviewed! ☺

In Solidarity,

Kryss Shane

Taking Self-Care Seriously

I was the kind of workaholic faculty member who was always there. I remember calling in to an "important" departmental committee meeting from my bed when I had strep throat. I remember having bronchitis and being told not to talk for three days; I couldn't possibly cancel class, so I went in and taught the lesson silently with a meme-filled PowerPoint. I remember once having a migraine, giving the students a small group activity in class, then going into the bathroom to vomit because of the pain. I've even had what the orthopedist called "spine flu" and later an unrelated tiny yet incredibly painful vascular hemorrhage in my intestines; both of these happened in early summer. My body had been keeping a record of my stress.

I'm not the only one to have put work above health and self-care. I heard stories from the women I interviewed about doing similar things. They were always sick like me but blew it off as allergies or just a cold until they couldn't avoid the truth any longer. Women dealing with undiagnosable muscle pain, gastrointestinal problems, and chronic fatigue. Lianne's is an extreme case, but one that many of us might relate to:

> I woke up one morning in terrible back pain. It felt like every nerve ending and muscle in my low back was seizing. I ended up having to be in the hospital for a few days and have a procedure. When we got the pain under control, all I could think was, I have these five meetings and my classes this week. So, between medical tests to make sure it was not something connected to others areas of my body, I was frantically trying to reach someone while I was in the hospital. I finally got in touch with the program director, who would, of course, cover my classes if I gave them access to my learning management system site and my lesson plan for the day. I gladly did it. I could barely sit up but made my partner bring me my computer. He was like, what are you doing? But he brought it, I got my lesson plans to the person taking over my

class, and I was grading papers from my hospital bed immediately after surgery. I was released three days later, and I should have stayed home, but the person covering my class was hinting that they couldn't do it forever. So I was back in the classroom the day after I was released. I could hardly walk. I look back thinking that was crazy. Why did I do that?

Why did she do it? Would I, or you, have done it? Before burnout, I probably would have. I thought I was lucky that my back and intestinal episodes happened in the summer. Part of the issue was boundaries, which I'll discuss, but I also wasn't connecting the body and the mind, not realizing that "wellness is not a sense of being, but a state of action" (Nagoski and Nagoski 2019, 28). Wellness is something we *do*. Self-care is something we must do regularly; it is more than the massage here and there or the occasional nap—though those are wonderful options in a longer-term self-care plan. One faculty member I spoke with, Jasmine, asks us to think more deeply about this connection:

This kind of mind-body separation is really diminishing to our lived experience in our bodies. It gets projected in a way that diminishes women and people of color, diminishes believed physical experience. It's also like you cut out a huge source of wisdom if you just think about cognition in the brain. So to me, a big part of thinking about burnout, which for me certainly had emotional and spiritual impact, is also really profound physical harm. I was thinking, what is the place and the value of the body? With all of the things that the body brings, it's not just necessarily an act of preservation, but also a possibility for really interesting kinds of creativity.

Whether physical or mental, rest, then, can be the most important step toward finding balance and enacting self-care.

Making Rest a Priority

When I say "rest," do you automatically think, "There's no time to rest, I have way too much to do"? Or maybe, "I can rest when this semester is over"? Or even just, "I rest; I have that monthly massage"? Rest isn't being lazy, nor is it something we can put off until the end of the semester or expect one massage or nap to address. Susanna Harris, a coach who works with graduate students and advocates for their mental health, told me that the students she works with don't "have the opportunity to burn out" or rest, because there is always something else to do:

> One of the reasons that we don't necessarily talk about it as much for grad students is that there's not really an opportunity to burn out on any one thing. Rather than having this introspection and saying, "Wow, I am really having a hard time right now," we can jump to another project. So as we get burnt out on one thing, all we have to do is say, "Okay, well, I'm not going to write right now. I'm going to go work in the lab." There's never this indication that if you find yourself getting really tired of one thing, and it turns out that this is affecting other work, you take a break. It's always, you go and do something else that's equally productive, but in a different way. And there's that massive amount of guilt attached to that.

But rest is not a gift or even a common practice that academic culture gives us: "You have to resist the lure of busyness, make time for rest, take it seriously, and protect it from a world that is intent on stealing it" (Pang 2018, 10). Resting doesn't mean just not looking at the article you're writing for a few days or not answering email immediately because if you are doing those things, you are still actively thinking about (not) working. The coach Jane Jones sees it all the time:

> Some people think if they only work this number of hours a week, they won't burn out. But if your brain is still going with the worry all the time, that's fatiguing you too, even if you think you have good boundaries because you don't work on weekends. If you're still worried about it after work, if you're still thinking about it, it's tiring you. I think that there's a lot of that type of fatigue that comes not necessarily from what people call action but just from all the thoughts we have that are tiring us.

A major component of good self-care is rest. Period, end of story. Rest. This might be sleep, that regular massage, or the kind of active rest that engages your mind with something totally different—like horses for me and meditation and hiking for others. Physically, true rest activates the default network mode in your mind, allowing the brain to recharge and process (Nagoski and Nagoski 2019, 158–61). In *How to Do Nothing* (2019), Jenny Odell argues that we should take "a break to just listen, to remember in the deepest sense of *what*, *when*, and *where* we are" (22). And returning to burnout directly, Padilla and Thompson (2016) found that "more social support, hours spent with family, hours spent on leisure activities, and hours spent sleeping are related to a decrease in burnout" (554).

But setting boundaries and protecting your rest and self means fighting a culture that expects more and more of you every year, every semester, every day. Cynthia Ganote explores how her body kept score when she didn't have good boundaries:

"I hate it when I have to let go! It's so hard. I don't like it!" I said to myself, in my most 12-year-old-girl voice.

It's confusing and painful in that moment when you start to feel the "Oh *no*. This has taken a turn" moment in your body, when your gut starts to churn, when it feels like your intestines are somehow, against the laws of gravity, starting to flip around and rearrange themselves into knots.

The situation is awful. It's hard. You get through it. And you think, "It's going to get better. It has to!" But it *does not* have to. It happens again. And then again. And again.

That bad feeling in your gut, it's amplified, it's reified, it's starting to institutionalize itself in there . . . and all of a sudden, as if in a genie's poof, the pattern is made clear. (Trust me, I'm a sociologist; I know a solid pattern when I see one.)

Merde.

I, like you, know from life when I'm getting the signal that it's time to let go. I know it, because my body tells me so. I don't *want* to know it in that moment, but I know it.

However, that's when I, perhaps also like you, *really* persist.

Because, "Nevertheless, she persisted!"

I'm that type. Are you?

But when to persist and when to let go? That one I'm not so good at.

While I was busy persisting no matter the cost to my body, mind, and spirit, my gut kept speaking to me again and again, making me progressively sicker.

At the same time, I developed a second enjoyable symptom, a cold anxiety sweat under my long, dark hair, no matter the temperature inside or out. The hair sweats came like clockwork every time I was about to walk into any space that I knew to be hostile territory, and they didn't let go of me.

Over time, what with my gut screaming and my hair dripping, I finally listened to my body. It took a very long time for me to admit that it was speaking to me, that I *knew* what I needed to do, that this environment was not a match for me, and it wasn't going to be.

Maybe *your* body uses another language: maybe it's those headaches, or that chronic adrenal problem, or the infernal insomnia. Maybe it's that feeling of a tightening in your chest, that feeling on a Sunday night that you *just cannot anymore*. Maybe it's the continual desire for sugar, or mac 'n' cheese, or fried foods, or a jug o' wine. Listen, I'm not judging! And I don't know your body. But I sure know mine, and my gut and hair are gonna sing like canaries when something isn't right, when the conditions aren't right for my thriving on an ongoing basis.

In the end, I realized that my body wasn't the affliction; the toxic situation I was in was the affliction. Though I wanted it to, my body wouldn't shut up and just *hang out* so I could enjoy my tenured faculty job in the fabulous Bay Area. I was super mad at its noncooperation, when I should've been thanking it every single day for giving me its knotty-churny messages.

In the end, I let go.

I'd be lying if I said that letting go was easy. It was the hardest thing I'd had to do in my life up to that point. But it had to be done, I was terrified while doing it, and I did it.

And that has made all the difference.

Setting Boundaries and Resisting Culture

I read Odell's book *How to Do Nothing* with both hope and skepticism. Learning how to "do nothing" had been one of the major recommendations from my therapist and psychiatrist when I began treatment for my burnout and the depression and anxiety that it reactivated. As I resisted that advice—why would I waste time when I should be writing or reading or grading?—it became painfully clear that I was terrified of doing nothing because I didn't know who I was when I *wasn't* doing. "Doing higher ed" defined me because I had become the embodiment of the culture of busyness and knew no boundaries to protect myself from overwork and burnout. If I was not doing, I was thinking, feeling guilty, or shaming myself about work.

Odell's book is surprisingly philosophical, making the radical argument that doing nothing is a statement against a culture that judges everything, including time and people, by economic measures. When viewed through the lens of academic capitalism, the culture of busyness both pushes us beyond the edge of reasonable personal and professional investment and leads us to believe that if we are not investing more and more work and pieces of ourselves, we are not worthy of higher ed. I, like Odell, call that bullshit, if you'll excuse my language. She says, "Nothing is harder than doing nothing. In a world where our value is determined by our productivity, many of us find our every last minute captured, optimized, or appropriated as a financial resource by the technologies we use daily" (ix).

When I talked to Roxanne, a faculty member in the social sciences, she reflected,

> I think for me what I thought academia was versus what it actually is was certainly a life lesson, but I think there's not any acknowledgment once you get so steeped in it. This isn't exactly a culture that's healthy,

or reasonable, or that compensates me in a way it should. When you start to get steeped in that, and then you are around others who don't ever acknowledge it, we normalize it. Right? So then it becomes, Oh, gosh, what's wrong with me that I don't want to work the entire weekend, or what's wrong with me because I haven't said yes to this additional committee, or why am I feeling this pressure to spend my own money to go to a conference? Because that's what I'm supposed to do.

Because that's what we are "supposed" to do. Susanna Harris told me this mind-set is instilled early in the graduate students she works with:

I don't think I've ever seen a graduate student on Twitter who hasn't felt guilty about taking a break or announced it as if it was a monumental accomplishment. Instead of just being like, "Hey, I took a break, and it was cool," many say things like "I was not brow beaten. I was not screamed at. I don't feel like the worst person in the world. It was hard. But come talk to me if you feel like it." Is this making it better? It's adding a whole other layer of "You see, I didn't feel guilty for setting this boundary for one weekend, but you may feel guilty, and I'm now better than you because I was able to take this weekend."

Brené Brown (2017) posits that "boundaries are hard when you want to be liked" (115), and I would add, when you are in higher ed. Email overload is an easy example of (not) setting boundaries based on perceived cultural norms. Coach Jane Jones told me about a client who felt obligated to respond to her email at all hours of the day and night because her senior colleagues were doing so. As they dug into the lack of boundaries in this one area, it ultimately became a conversation about self-care. Jones suggested the client work her way up to limiting email hours to specific times of the day because she deserved it: she deserved quiet time to do whatever she wanted—to write, read, watch Netflix, relax—and she deserved not to have to be accountable to other people every minute of the day.

Jones's approach mirrors Brown's caution about not having boundaries. "People learn to treat us based on how they see us treating ourselves," writes Brown. "If I don't put value on my work or my time, neither will the person I am helping. Boundaries are a function of self-respect and love" (2017, 129). Jennifer Snodgrass invites us to consider our boundaries intentionally:

> *Leave your office.* This is a tough lesson that took me almost a decade to embrace. It is okay to leave your office for an extended period. You do not have to be in the middle of it all at all times. Even if it means taking your papers to the library across campus for grading or meeting a colleague for a business lunch, step away from your computer and your desk. There's a lot to be said for ten minutes of fresh air. Leaving the confines of your academic building is good for productivity, colleague relationships, and your own disposition. I'm still working on this one.
>
> *Flattery is fun, but know the truth behind it.* Any member of the academy can get swept up in praise and adoration. To be honest, validation for our work is incredibly important, and we thrive on it. However, when you are flattered *continually* by colleagues or upper administration, realize there's a chance something is behind the actions. Flattery causes you to say yes more often and to listen to others' agendas rather than your own ideas. Do not confuse flattery with friendship and support. I have plenty of colleagues I go to for validation and can now recognize when someone is feeding me a line to get me to do something.
>
> *Say no, and mean it.* I have learned that people expect an excuse immediately after you say no. Statements such as "No, I can't

be on the search committee because I have a major grant to complete" or "No, I won't be able to be at the meeting tomorrow because I am giving a presentation at that time" are common within academic circles. But what if we chose another response, such as "Thank you, but that's just not an option." I'm always amazed by this phrase as it truly doesn't give the other party a chance to respond. There are no excuses, you don't have to provide a why. "Thank you, but that's not an option" simply stops the conversation.

And Sharon Mitchler takes boundary-setting advice a step further for full-time faculty:

Know the limits of your stated workload. What does your job description include? Equally important, what does it omit? If it is not in the job description, you may refer to that document when you are determining your workload with department chairs and administrators. If you have a negotiated agreement or contract, it should identify limits and boundaries. You need to know those boundaries so that you are not pulled into doing more work, or work of a different type, than you should.

In order to protect your professional boundaries, you have to know them. Remember, we tend to do a lot of independent goal setting and management of our own workflow. Academic peers and above are not necessarily trying to overwork you, but they are all trying to do more with less. They are not keeping track of the rest of your work. Other people will not know that you are already developing two new classes when they ask you to develop another new class, or that you are already writing a human subject research protocol, or have three drafts of publications in progress.

What are the upper limits of your workload? How many committees are you expected to serve on? What service requirements are identified? What does *other duties as assigned* mean on your campus? When you know these details, you may more clearly determine when to decline or put off an opportunity.

If possible, minimize your need to work moonlighting gigs, summers, extended contracts. One way to avoid burnout is to refuse to work extra when you don't want to. This may not be possible, but if you can, decide what your time is worth. If it is not possible to take time away—summers, for example—be sure to plan for specific times when you don't work. Work best first thing in the morning? Then make the afternoons non-work hours. Need to coordinate with someone else? Then plan not to do all the prep work alone and decide how tasks will be divided up. If you are always the one who takes minutes or records progress, stop it. Just stop it. Demand that someone else carry that load too. Rotate the responsibility if you must, but avoid doing *all* the legwork whenever possible. When you run into a group that seems to be happy to let you do all the heavy lifting, remember to saying no.

Working all the time takes time away from family, friends, community and social events, leisure and pastimes, even just staring at the wall daydreaming. As Odell writes, "The point of doing nothing, as I define it, isn't to return to work refreshed and ready to be more productive, but rather to question what we currently perceive as productive" (2019, xii).

How can you set better boundaries to protect yourself from or help you deal with burnout? Jennifer Marlow offers one plan.

Jenny Odell's book *How to Do Nothing: Resisting the Attention Economy* (2019) calls on each of us to resist capitalism by regaining control over our attention. Our attention, after all, is our reality, and it is also, Odell argues, a hot commodity. We are seduced by the mechanisms of the "attention economy." False consciousness appears to have a firm grasp, as we happily craft status updates, pins, snaps, captioned photos, YouTube videos, and the like. We are at once producer and consumer, making us a valuable unpaid asset to the owning class. With all of this unpaid labor in addition to our work within the corporate structure of higher education, it is no small wonder that we are suffering burnout. To counter this, Odell offers the ideas of "standing apart" and "resistance-in-place" as means of gaining control over and effectively withholding our attention.

When it comes to the attention economy, Odell tells us, it is important to "know your enemy." The enemy most likely differs from person to person, and so each resistance-in-place plan will look a little different. The first thing you will want to pinpoint is your enemy (or enemies, more likely): What are the things that steal your attention? What parts of your job draw your attention in a way that makes you feel more cog than person? What aspects of your life or job divide your attention in ways that exhaust you? Pinpointing these enemies is the first step in creating your standing-apart plan. It might also be useful to note which of the things you named you can actually let go of while maintaining employment and which you truly need to pay attention to in order to stay employed.

The next step is to choose a person who will help hold you accountable to your resistance-in-place plan. Preferably this person will be a colleague—someone who is familiar with your specific institutional culture and attention enemies—but it can be anyone you trust to hold you to the work of regaining control over your attention. Together—or separately is fine too—develop a list of ways that you can more purposefully direct your attention, ways that resist the attention economy. Consider the "attention enemies" you have and think about what you want to replace them with. To give some concrete examples, I share my friend Tara's and my simplified lists. We have recorded these lists in a shared spreadsheet with columns for entering the date we commit to enacting them, a section to record the outcome (how it went, what we learned, etc.), and a column to indicate that we've checked in with each other (see the box for a partial spreadsheet).

While making shared spreadsheets, being in regular communication with someone, creating lists, and then following through on planned actions might feel like its own form of work, the key to countering burnout might not be the traditional modes of self-care and relaxation that we think of (vacations, spa days, yoga classes, binge-watching shows, etc.). If we believe that capitalism itself is the culprit for burnout, and if the places where we work are themselves increasingly corporatized, then it seems to follow that actively resisting corporate, and academic, capitalism is a crucial step toward combating burnout. This takes work.

Tara's attention enemies:	Jenn's attention enemies:
• Compulsively checking real-estate listings • Online shopping • (True crime) podcasts • Social media (Twitter)	• Her own mind • Obsessively checking email without the intent to thoughtfully respond • Social media • News intake
Tara and Jenn's shared list of ways to (re)direct attention:	
• Space- or place-based walk with no devices/headphones • Reading, contemplation, and teatime • No devices after [*time*] or no devices between [*time*] and [*time*] • *Guilt-free* time off from work for meditation, yoga, and rest • No news after [*time*] or no news between [*time*] and [*time*]	

Getting a Hobby

One means of directing our attention away from all-consuming work to be present in the world is to have a hobby or pastime. It feels silly to write that. "Get a hobby." But finding and engaging in an activity that focuses your attention on the present, doing something for no other reason than the pleasure it brings you and the state of flow you can achieve, is powerful. In Aristotle's ethics, good lives were a combination of work to sustain one's livelihood and leisure to sustain the soul. Balance, then, is fed by both engagement in our work and active attention to things like family and friends, hobbies, travel, and simply reading for pleasure, "aspects of our lives that make us uniquely human: our souls, our minds, our personal and civic relationships (Hall 2018, 184–85).

My husband has been telling me for pretty much our entire twenty-year relationship that I need a hobby. A software engineer by trade, he has hobbies that work a different part of his brain, the part of him that could easily have been a mechanical engineer. He can get so absorbed in these activities that it's near sacrilege to interrupt him for little things like dinner. I've had various almost-hobbies over the years, riding obviously, but also things like jewelry making, that direct all of my focus into the act of communing with the horse or creating something new out of stones and wire.

In the Aristotelian sense, as well as a psychological sense, these engrossing leisure activities are a form of active rest, of divorcing oneself from work and getting lost in an activity that engages a different part of the brain. Like physical movement, an engrossing activity can restore some of the wells of energy and care exhausted by burnout. Pang (2018) summarizes twenty years of work by the German sociologist Sabine Sonnentag, saying, "Workers who have the chance to get away mentally, switch off, and devote their energies elsewhere, are more productive, have better attitudes, get along better with their colleagues, and are better able to deal with challenges at work" (165). So while "doing nothing" might feel unnatural, active rest and deep, absorbing play feed the parts of us that can resist burnout.

Some of the women I spoke with engaged in this deep refreshing play:

Shantal had grown up competing in a hockey league. She eventually stopped competing and moved on to graduate work. As she entered midcareer malaise, she pulled out her skates and started to practice again, not for competition but just for herself.

Anya works out her stress doing and teaching aerial yoga, the kind done with silks hanging from the ceiling like in Cirque du Soleil shows. The beauty of the physical movements calms her body and soul.

Linda is a constant knitter. Now a senior faculty member, she even knits in meetings to temper her sometimes too honest comments. She finds joy knitting blankets and sweaters for local nursing home residents.

Toya is a foodie. She loves to cook and regularly attends gourmet chef competitions with a group of women who share a similar love for creative recipes and unique plating strategies.

Tapping these other aspects of themselves allows each to practice leisure purposively, so as Aristotle might say, it was not wasted time at all (Hall 2018, 185).

The psychologist Dina Gohar and I had a conversation about hobbies:

> DG: I think of it in terms of treatment approach. It's very similar to treating a depression or a mix of depression and anxiety. We have to figure out what you actually enjoy doing, what we can actually

help you find joy in. And then, if it's things that you do enjoy but you're no longer seeing as valuable because academia, we deal with that. For some reason, we only value writing our papers and publishing and when the burnout comes, we think, who cares if I play music or do this or do that? I should be writing. The pandemic has heightened that in some ways because people are actually forced to find these hobbies to stay busy.

My hobbies are pretty much not possible because of COVID because I go out to eat at nice places, to travel, to theater and concerts. So I had to think maybe I should learn some activity. Or am I interested in joining a singing group? It has actually helped more than I thought it would just because singing itself, it's just very rejuvenating, maybe because you're forced to do deep breathing. So it's finding ways to get yourself out of that fight or flight and focus your attention wholly on something else.

RPR: I was reading a book and the author said we don't have pastimes anymore because we don't pass time, we spend it. A lot of us don't really have hobbies. My husband races motorcycles, so there's always something in the garage he can do and find a flow state. For me, for a while it was horses. But then I got to a point where I was taking lessons and I didn't feel I was "progressing" fast enough. And I'm watching little kids be able to do the things that I couldn't do. And the burnout voice got to me: "I'm never going to compete* because I'm terrible and too old to do this. This is a total waste of time and money. What am I doing here? I should be writing."

DG: I can relate to that logic for sure. Oh, I'm not going to end up being a singer. So why do I need to make time for that? Yeah, exactly.

---

* Which I never wanted to do in the first place. I just wanted to hang out with horses.

RPR: Agreed. It's funny now thinking back on it, because when I started riding I didn't know anything. I just wanted to have something to do, and horses are fun to be around. They emote with you, they empathize with you, and you can build a connection there. I just wanted to do something, and I'm not an outdoorsy person. So it was very weird to be with horses, but it made me happy, until the burnout started talking.

DG: A lot of academics lose our hobbies over time. I had hobbies going into grad school, and I started singing in grad school for a little while. But after two years I started to think, Oh, I don't have my evenings anymore. Oh, I used to have this ridiculous, natural, decent range and all these things, but because it's been so long I can't do this. But then when I started again recently, I actually feel better. Why does it have to be that I have to sing flawlessly in order for that to be time well spent? It's that reframe. It's not about doing something well, it's about doing something and enjoying it and it's okay if you suck at it. And that growth mind-set piece of it, maybe it's actually good to suck at something and actually just experience that cause it's okay.

RPR: And that's definitely something that I would preach to my students. Go ahead and bomb something or take this pottery class knowing you're going to totally suck at it, just so you know. It's a different way to use your brain.

Coach Hillary Hutchinson finds this strategy of cross-fertilization to be extremely valuable for her clients as well.

Burnout is frequently the reason academics in higher education call me for coaching. The feeling of burnout may be so intense that all these clients can think about is, how do I get out of academia?

Escape from academia is not always the right answer; instead, consider changing what you do outside work using a strategy I call cross-fertilization.

Cross-fertilization is a way to avoid burnout and is far more active than relaxation. People suffering from burnout are often advised to "get a massage" or "give yourself a day off" to help them find their way to "work-life balance." My advice is to engage in a fun and interesting activity *away from* the demands of the academy. Cross-fertilization can make a huge difference in an academic's life and well-being, as the goal is to find a way to fill your well and feed your soul.

You do not need to turn your life upside down and drop out of your current work to engage in some major alternative activity like hiking the Appalachian Trail or joining a monastery. Instead, engage in small activities outside your current comfort zone and work life for restoration. Have you always wanted to try a martial art but been afraid you didn't have the physical capability? Find a class and try it out. Have you always wanted to play a musical instrument but been afraid of embarrassing yourself? Find a music teacher and take some private lessons. Have you always wanted to learn how to can fruits and vegetables? Check out your local farmer's market to see if someone there would be willing to teach you. The activity you pick doesn't really matter, as long as it is something you really want to do but have never done. It must be truly interactive, not passive.

Whatever you pick might be a little bit uncomfortable at first. Give yourself permission to take the time to do something not directly related to your academic work. Put yourself in a growth mind-set (see Dweck 2016). Cross-fertilization is meant to take you into uncharted territory. Successful cross-fertilization means finding an activity that inspires, renews, stimulates, or encourages the restoration of balance in a work life that's out of balance. New activities approached from the position of "this is an experiment" or with a lighthearted sense of play and fun are more likely to be antidotes to obligation and work. Cross-fertilization activities help avoid burnout.

- What are *three* things you've never done but would like to try? (It's okay to include ideas that seem far-fetched right now.)
- What did you enjoy doing as a child? (Consider what it would be like to do this as an adult.)
- What are you doing right now for fun and recreation? (If the answer is nothing, find something you can start doing *now*, whether it is going to a movie or a walk in the park.)

It doesn't matter what the hobby is as long as it's healthy, fun, and engaging. The best pastimes that help regulate burnout are ones that help you reach a state of flow or use a completely different part of your brain. What might work for you in terms of a hobby or pastime you can turn your attention to as you form boundaries and bring balance in your life? What interests might you explore, or what classes might you take? What could you suck at and enjoy as a beginner? Self-care, boundaries, and hobbies can ultimately be paths to purpose, compassion, and connection.

Conclusion

It's been more than a year since I sat on that veranda watching the horses graze and trail around the woods with Billy. I've been back a few times since then to relax and commune. Since moving to a larger city, I haven't had much opportunity to ride, but I'm okay with that for now. I still enjoy reading and watching anything equestrian, like the horse-crazy little girls I met at the barn.

As I wrap up this chapter and the book, I leave you with these questions:

- What would the opposite of burnout look like for you?
- How are you prioritizing elements of your life and work?
- What do you do when you aren't "doing" higher ed?
- How do you know when you are out of balance?
- What can help you feel or stay balanced?
- What changes might you see in your life if you were more balanced?

Where can you go from here—where do you want to go, and how do you want to get there? Consider exploring purpose, compassion, connection, and balance.

Coda

I'm standing at my desk in my home office shifting from foot to foot as I wait for Laura to join our video call. It's been three years since our first meeting, when I first heard the word *burnout* used in relation to me and my struggles. So much has happened in those three years. I finally dealt with decades of pain I'd been squashing. I left my tenured faculty role at a medium-sized liberal arts–focused institution for a non-tenure-track position in faculty development at a large state technical institute. I'm working on a coaching certification with the goal of supporting women faculty facing challenges related to higher ed life, including burnout. I also started a podcast interviewing women I admire in and around higher ed.

It was all hard work. Hard. Work. I've made peace with RPR and am mentally and emotionally stronger than I have ever been. And I'm enjoying my work and projects.

Sometimes I wonder if I'll fall into burnout again, but Laura and I agree I'm a different person now. My values have changed, my identity is my own, and I have a much healthier balance between work, life, and rest. My purpose in my higher ed work is no longer weighed down by all the shoulds and have-tos. I know how to act with compassion toward myself and others. I feel more connected to my colleagues and peers, as well as to some amazing people I've met on social media. And if I want to play Solitaire on my phone for an hour after a day of work, I do.

Writing this book and hearing these women's stories and advice has changed me as well. I know now that my experience with burnout, once so shameful to me, was not singular. I stand in solidarity with these women and the ones who could not or were not ready to share their stories. I'm grateful for the advice and perspective provided by the psychologists, coaches, and faculty developers who contributed to the book as well.

And I know we have to do the work to change the culture of higher ed. I'm here for it and hope you are as well.

A chime interrupts my musing, and I hear Laura's singsong greeting, "Hello-oo, how are you?"

"I'm really good," I say. "I finished the book."

Acknowledgments

My sincere thanks to the contributors, both named and anonymous, for sharing their stories with such vulnerability and wisdom and helping to open this conversation about burnout.

Thank you to the colleagues and coaches I interviewed for their perspectives on burnout among women in higher ed: Dina Gohar, Kristina Hallett, Jane Jones, Michelle Dionne Thompson, and Fatimah Williams. Thanks, as well, to Brooke Clubbs for bouncing ideas around with me. Special thanks to Katie Linder for her insight and encouragement when I needed another perspective.

I'm indebted to the blind reviewers who took the time to review the proposal and manuscript as well as to the generous readers who previewed the book or proposal and offered generative feedback: Mary Churchill, Francine Glazer, Mandi Martyn, and Kara Taczak. Extra thanks to Danielle Apfelbaum for her detailed and substantive feedback.

I want to extend my thanks to my colleagues and leaders at Elon University for their support and encouragement during my burnout period, for accepting my plight as real and not imagined, and for allowing me to put my mental health first even when it put work back on their plates.

To my ever-supportive, encouraging, and committed editor, Greg Britton, your faith in me and this book kept me going when I was sure I was writing the wrong book. You were right; it is the right book.

My deepest and most heartfelt thanks go to my therapist, Laura Ellington. Laura was with me from the very beginning, helping me to discover and recover from burnout. We broke RPR down and built her back up as a new me. I came up with the idea for this book in therapy, at the time thinking it was just my academic brain trying to turn pain into work, but this one had legs. The book wouldn't exist without the work we did, and I am forever grateful.

And finally, thanks to my family, especially my husband, Tracey, for taking care of me when I couldn't take care of myself, loving me when I couldn't love myself, anchoring me when I wanted to float away, and putting up with me in writing mode.

Appendix I

Special Advice
for Educational Developers

Legacy Reflection as an Antidote to Burnout

CATHERINE ROSS AND KRISTI VERBEKE

Over the course of an academic career, faculty move through distinctive and commonly shared phases: from the early years to midcareer and late career (Baldwin, Lunceford, and Vanderlinden 2005). The pressures and challenges of each career phase have been identified by researchers, but few faculty have time to actually reflect on their career paths in the day-to-day bustle of the teaching, research, and service duties that form the foundation of faculty life. Yet reflection on one's career is vital to remaining engaged and to being able to keep challenges of any particular time period in perspective.

Opportunities for reflection are critical in the later years of faculty careers, when faculty often take on more leadership and administrative roles to support their institutions (D. T. Hall 1986) and assist their departments and institutions in addressing the myriad struggles that are common to higher education today: enrollment drops, budget cuts, campus climate, aging campus infrastructure, etc. The burnout among senior faculty is palpable in the cynicism, fear, and anger that faculty voice when given the safe space to share.

LEGACY AS A FRAMING DEVICE FOR CAREER REFLECTION

The need for time to reflect on one's career is broadly suggested in Erik Erikson's Stages of Identity Development schema for both the middle-age and older-adulthood stages (see Erikson 1969), both of which focus on meaning making and purpose (Karpiak 1997, 25):

- Mid-Life—Generativity vs. stagnation

  Does the middle-aged adult find purpose and meaning in his life?

  (Virtue: caring)

- Old Age—Ego integrity vs. despair

  Is the older-aged adult satisfied with her values and life's accomplishments?

  (Virtue: wisdom)

When we designed a teaching-renewal retreat directly targeting mid- and late-career faculty, we created an opportunity for career reflection with an opening and closing legacy-reflection activity, resulting in a bookending of perspective taking on academic careers from the vantage point of decades. For the purposes of supporting the retreat theme of teaching renewal, the main focus of the legacy reflection was professional legacy, but many participants found it difficult to separate personal from professional, especially when thinking about teaching. Since teaching is a relationship-based endeavor, contrasting with the often solo endeavors of research and writing, this was not particularly surprising, so we kept the parameters open to whatever the participants wished to include in their legacy ideas.

The Legacy Activity

The opening legacy reflection used the following questions:

- What professional legacies am I leaving?
- Are they tangible or intangible?
- Are they intentional or unintentional?
- How am I creating/nurturing them?
- Are they what I want to leave?

In the closing legacy reflection, participants were encouraged to commit to a more concrete plan:

- What two professional legacies do I want to actively work on leaving?
- How will I create and nurture them?
- What support/resources (people/knowledge/skills/experience) do I need to achieve them?
- How can I help others create legacies that are meaningful to them? How can I support others' legacies?

Legacy reflection provided faculty with a way to make meaning of their careers, their teaching, and their relationship with their institutions. In combination with the other parts of the retreat, it was a powerful catalyst for renewal, change, and creating an intentional path forward in the latter years of their careers.

Professors Are People Too! Retrieving "Selfishness" as a Way to Avoid Burnout

EMILY O. GRAVETT

Oddly, the ultimate focus of much professional development programming is not the faculty members themselves but the students. This focus reveals itself subtly, but in numerous and pervasive ways, such as the recommendation, common in one-off workshops and more immersive course-design institutes, that faculty write syllabi that feel warm, welcoming, invitational, and promising—to the students (see, e.g., Bain 2004; and Harnish and Bridges 2011); the innovative efforts launched to solicit students' voices and perspectives about instruction, through Small-Group Instructional Diagnosis or more long-term student-faculty partnerships (Cook-Sather, Bovill, and Felten 2014); the concern that there be clear, integrated, and significant outcomes for students that span the learning domains (Fink 2013); or the decades-long push to make classrooms more learning- and even learner-centered (Weimer 2013).

While understandable, even laudable, such an emphasis on the students across institutions of higher education—that is, an emphasis on their learning, their personal development, their safety, their sense of belonging, their identities, their extracurriculars, their mental health, their employability, etc.—has the potential to distance or decenter faculty members from the educational process. It may inadvertently lead faculty to neglect themselves (or worse, to feel like they *should* neglect themselves), prioritizing their students and what is best for their students above all else. Such neglect can, as I've witnessed, result in stress, guilt, being overwhelmed, and burnout. Yet faculty are people who matter too.

I'll say it again for those in the back: faculty are people who matter too!

As an educational developer (and a faculty member), I find myself frequently having to remind colleagues of this fact. For instance, one pre-tenure professor I recently met with had several thoughtful, exciting, well-evidenced ideas for how to make an upcoming course more student-centered, more active and interactive, more scaffolded, more transparent. They were wonderful ideas. And they would have required an enormous amount of labor on her part to successfully implement. Yet it soon came out in our conversation that she would only be offering this course one semester. All of that time and effort would benefit one relatively small group of students. That's it. I suggested to her that maybe totally revamping a course to teach it only one semester might not be the best use of *her* time—not least because she had other courses in rotation that she was also passionate about and ready to attend to. She was visibly relieved when I gave her permission to consider herself in this casual cost-benefit calculation.

Yet I do not hear these kinds of *faculty*-focused considerations widely mentioned or even encouraged in professional development opportunities. I worry that the implication instructors absorb—their main takeaway—is that they should be doing whatever it takes if it's good for the students, even if it's to their own detriment . . . and that they are bad teachers if that's not what they're doing. Student learning isn't the only consideration in the teaching nexus.

Just as parents sometimes need to take care of themselves first (e.g., by exercising, going on date nights, etc.) in order to be the best parents they can be, so too do faculty. Therefore, I'd like to retrieve a certain notion of selfishness so that faculty feel empowered to consider themselves centrally in their own teaching decisions and practices, for themselves (and, perhaps, for their students).

Here are some questions faculty might ask themselves as you work with them to be "selfish":

- What are your values and priorities? How well does this teaching-related work align with those?
- What do you feel excited to be focused on? What motivates you?
- How much time and effort will this new course, assignment, activity, etc., take you to design and implement? How many students will benefit from your labor, now and in the future?
- What else do you have on your plate professionally?
- What else do you have on your plate personally? How do these affect the time, energy, and emotion that you have to devote to work?
- Why are you doing this?
- What can you say no to?
- No, really, what can you say no to?

Making teaching-related decisions that consider or even sometimes *prioritize* yourself is just fine. It may be key to avoiding the faculty burnout that so plagues higher education.

Burning the Candle at Both Ends: Supporting the Multiplicity of Faculty Roles

SANDA SGOUTAS-EMCH

It's become a badge of honor in today's driven society to push the envelope and burn the candles at both ends, but you can only do this so long before you flame out.

—Dr. Edward Creagan, Mayo Clinic

For educational developers, the responsibility of supporting faculty success weighs heavily on our minds, especially when we meet with faculty who are stressed and feel underappreciated. Much like therapists (but without the license), educational developers are exposed to personal stories from faculty about bullying, harassment, inequities, unfair practices, and general unhappiness. Intersect these stories with the demands of faculty's own personal life circumstances and you have a potential for accelerated burnout. Faculty who have children with special needs, for example, may face many physical and mental demands, such as dealing with doctors, school systems, and psychologists, and making time to go to appointments, which add to their daily stress. Other common examples of external factors include taking care of elderly parents, managing chronic illness, and relationship problems.

The question is, how might we more holistically assist faculty during these tumultuous times? It is a balancing act to maintain self-care and performance given the culture of higher education and personal demands from home (Hubbard, Atkins, and Brinko 1998; Richards, Andrew, and Levesque-Bristol 2016). However, these faculty are not alone. This minichapter explores ways to help faculty deal with both ends of the candle by discussing how to connect faculty and create solutions together based on my own experiences working with faculty in these circumstances.

Approaching faculty burnout using various strategies to support connection between those describing similar circumstances is essential for success and retention of faculty (Rook 2015). In addition, finding ways to support faculty as they attend to their well-being through self-care is just as important (Roesner et al. 2012). The following suggestions are based on the work done while I was serving as the director of my institution's faculty development center. These strategies, which are focused on forming connections and self-care, are easily applied at any type of institution and require few, if any, resources. Of course, in the end we might not be able to avoid burnout in all individuals, but these suggestions should help minimize the negative impact of a life in academia on those who are also experiencing stress and anxiety as a result of personal circumstances.

FORMING AFFINITY GROUPS

Affinity groups are formal or informal groups formed around a shared interest or common goal. These types of groups have been institutionalized in a range of work environments (Van Aken, Monetta, and Sink 1994). Affinity groups are often social in nature and can provide a much-needed space for individuals who belong to often marginalized communities in the academy, such as faculty of color and LGBTQ+ faculty. For example, at my own institution we work with our human resources department and the Center for Inclusive Excellence to create a confidential affinity group for faculty and staff who identify as members of the LGBTQ+ community. Given that our institution is Catholic, members of this community often feel added pressure because of their sexual orientation and gender expression. The campus can be perceived as an unsafe space for those who are out. The confidential affinity group serves as a safe space for many and a needed retreat for those who are anxious about how their identity might be perceived by others and impact their success at the institution.

CREATING COMMUNITIES OF PRACTICE AND LEARNING COMMUNITIES

Communities of practice and learning communities are developmental opportunities for faculty and staff to engage in meaningful conversations about various topics and to create both learning and supportive spaces for those who participate.

Two examples from my own institution came about because of faculty members' interest and need based on their personal and professional roles. The first example is a community we created for faculty who have children with special needs. This group meets twice a semester to discuss their life circumstances and coping methods. We also invite special guests, such as disability advocates and special education experts, to speak with the community and provide much-needed information. The faculty and staff who are members also engage in conversations on Universal Design for Learning and how UDL principles can be applied to classrooms as well as at home. The open space to talk about issues but also the time taken to educate those who may not be aware of the resources available is comforting to those who attend.

The second example is a mindfulness group for faculty who were feeling overwhelmed, lost, or marginalized. Although different from a support group, this community meets to discuss various mindfulness techniques and strategize how to overcome some of their work and home issues (Gorski 2015). Mindfulness is thought to help develop habits of mind associated with resilience

(Roesner et al. 2012). Providing an opportunity for faculty to exchange knowledge about various mindfulness techniques and the space to practice those techniques gives these individuals a well-needed respite from their day-to-day lives. The space is also used for discussing some of the home and work issues that are frequent stressors and to brainstorm about how to handle that stress.

Connection with Others during a Focused Retreat Experience

CATHERINE ROSS AND KRISTI VERBEKE

Our effort to combat faculty burnout comes in the form of a three-day teaching-renewal retreat designed as a holistic renewal effort for midcareer faculty. The structure of the retreat is influenced by the work of Rendón (2009) in that it offers participants opportunities to explore contemplative practices in addition to more traditional educational development programming, such as workshops and book discussions. The underlying values of the retreat are caring, safety, and support (Ross 2015). We also integrate best practices from the faculty learning community literature by encouraging small-group, interdisciplinary, cross-institutional participation (Cox and Richlin 2004). Participation is voluntary and noncompetitive (applications are accepted in the order they are received). The retreat is led by four or five educational developers who serve as workshop and peer-group facilitators. A sample schedule can be found in Ross 2015.

RETREAT CORE ELEMENTS

Although we framed the retreat around teaching, it includes several activities that contribute to renewal.

Accommodations and facilities that encourage reflection and make participants feel valued. The Graylyn Teaching Renewal Retreat, hosted by Wake Forest University, was named for its location, the Graylyn Inn and Conference Center in Winston Salem, North Carolina. Graylyn is a historic home with lush grounds and an extremely attentive staff. Participants often express appreciation for the facility and its staff and directly connect the location to their feelings of renewal. One participant wrote, "The location of the retreat was exquisite.... The staff of Graylyn was exceedingly friendly, and the food and the physically beautiful environment supported the 'retreat' feel" (Ross 2015).

Legacy as an anchor for the retreat. Over the years we have refined the opening and closing activity and have settled on using the idea of one's legacy to bookend the retreat. (The legacy reflection questions and activities were originally designed by by Kate Brinko, of Appalachian State, and adapted over the years.) We begin the retreat by introducing the idea of legacy as a way to align one's academic career. At the beginning as well as at the end of the retreat, participants reflect on the personal and professional legacies they want to leave.

Peer working groups. Participants are divided into small (6–8), interdisciplinary, cross-institutional peer working groups. As part of the retreat application, they are asked to submit a case study detailing a current challenge they are experiencing with respect to teaching. Each day, participants meet with their peer group, led by a retreat facilitator, and take turns processing their case studies. The effect of these working groups is powerful; 81 percent of participants identify them as the most valuable component of the retreat. They feel safe and cared for by their colleagues during these group interactions, citing deep exchanges and an atmosphere that encourages honest sharing and collaboration (Ross 2015).

Book discussions. All participants are asked to read *How Learning Works*, by Susan Ambrose and colleagues (2010), prior to attending the retreat. During the retreat, we designate time to discuss the book, and principles from the book are often integrated into other activities, such as the peer working groups and workshops.

Workshops. We offer workshops focused around themes of reflection and innovation in teaching throughout the retreat. Topics have included contemplative practices in teaching, teaching today's student, integrating simple technologies, Just-In-Time (JIT) teaching, creating engaging assignments and in-class activities, and motivating ourselves. Like the book discussions, these workshops are intended to help faculty increase their knowledge and self-efficacy around teaching.

Self-reflection. In an effort to make this a true retreat for participants, we build in time for self-reflection, or "down" time, each day after lunch. We encourage participants to use this time in a way that best serves them. We see them engaging in a variety of activities, including taking advantage of the beautiful grounds of Graylyn by going on walks, reading, visiting informally with other participants, taking naps, to recharge. This participant's comment expresses appreciation for the pacing of the retreat, including this targeted self-reflection time: "All pieces worked well together, including the breaks and opportunities for walks, naps and informal exchanges" (Ross 2015).

Wellness activities. In an effort to make this a truly holistic, renewal experience for participants, we offer a variety of wellness activities throughout the day, including yoga, walking, meditation, and tai chi. Our hope is that in addition to receiving care from colleagues and retreat facilitators, participants will be intentional about engaging in their own self-care while at the retreat.

Personal coaching. Participants are also given an optional opportunity to engage in coaching sessions, led by a certified coaching professional. These sessions have been conducted at the individual and the group level over the years. The emphasis is on the fulfillment of participants' personal and professional potential.

WHY A RETREAT TO COMBAT BURNOUT?

Undoubtedly, there are many approaches to combating faculty burnout. We feel the retreat format can be especially beneficial because of its intense focus. Rather than engaging in semester- or year-long programming, faculty are given the opportunity to participate in a way that allows them to disconnect from the demands of everyday life and focus deeply on renewal in a supportive, caring environment. Structured with a variety of activities that specifically encourage renewal, faculty receive much needed support from others, build efficacy around their academic skills, and reflect on the personal and professional legacy they want to leave.

Appendix 2

Bonus Interviews

Katie Linder

RPR: I'm curious about what themes related to burnout you see in your coaching practice, particularly with your academic women clients.

KL: In terms of themes, the thing that immediately comes to mind is clients who are experiencing confusion. They have found themselves here in their careers, usually midcareer to senior career, and it is not feeling meaningful to them. They are feeling overwhelmed, or they are just feeling apathetic about where things are going; nothing feels exciting anymore.

When you begin an academic career—and I'm talking primarily about faculty in kind of traditional roles, but I think this can apply more broadly—there is a set of expectations, of hoops that you jump through to move from one level to another level, and some people I think really enjoy the clarity of that. Even though the tenure and promotion process isn't always clear, this concept of going from here to here to here to here is relatively consistent across institutions. And I think that people enjoy that.

But then they get far enough along that they start ask to themselves, Is this it? Is this everything?, and that's usually when they show up for coaching. They've gotten to that point where they're no longer feeling fulfilled and start to question if they ever really were fulfilled. Maybe they didn't feel fulfilled all along but were busy doing the hoop jumping.

That hoop jumping is a form of a value system that higher education gives us about achievement, about niching, about what it means to contribute to a field or a discipline, and sometimes those values don't match an individual's value system. But they take the values on because that's what they think they have to do in order to be successful within higher ed. So, a lot of the pattern I see is people starting to feel a misalignment, but they don't understand that it's a misalignment, and so they're confused. They're not recognizing what exactly is causing that feeling of misalignment, so we often go down the pathway of talking about values.

RPR: In conversations that I've had with women experiencing burnout, they refer to their career paths as hamster wheels that just keep going and keep getting tighter and tighter because you have so many things to do. And they often say, "I just don't know why I'm doing it anymore. I feel like I'm doing all of these things that people are asking me to do, but just because I think I should be or I'm supposed to do things, am I getting any fulfillment for that?" It's the expectation escalation. The bar keeps moving.

KL: Agreed, and for some people that is satisfying. I also think that there is, for some academics, a point where their own expectations start to relax because they've figured it out. In the beginning, it's all just trying to figure it out. In grad school, it feels so mysterious. There's so much tacit knowledge that you don't really feel like you're ever going to know, and then at some point you do and it's like the wizard behind the curtain, you know: this is all there is? Many tell me they thought they would feel a level of meaningfulness that they don't feel. It's a surprise because they thought once they hit this or that milestone they would be satisfied. Yet they're not, so what do you do with that?

RPR: It can be a big disappointment for some when they realize that that's all that's there, and part of the culture is the value system in which we never learn to be content with anything or any achievement. There's always a level up. There's always a next step.

It reminds me of the idea of perpetual growth culture. Our culture talks about always growing. We should always be learning something or doing something or growing in some way; there's no appreciation just for stasis because every moment is pushing toward my personal growth or my professional growth. That's obviously the part of the academic capitalism idea that time is money and we should feel guilty for not using time for work. That sounded powerful to me—that you don't have to be growing every moment of every day.

KL: I would also layer in that some people come to higher ed because they have a deep value of personal and professional growth or lifelong learning, and what they're finding in higher ed is not aligned with that, you know, like it's kind of a surface-level understanding of that. Some people are redefining their values of working and what it means to do things on your own time. What does it mean to explore something just because you want to explore it? I think that for a lot of academics that can be confusing because they do have a value around learning but just never really embraced it as a very personal, centering value to themselves. They've just kind of assumed it was the job, and it's not necessarily that. It's separating out your personal and professional values from the values that are imbued within your job. Sometimes there's overlap there when we're lucky and aligned, but not always.

There's so much self-awareness that's needed for these discussions, and if you've never been asked to engage in that level of self-awareness and reflection, it feels so foreign and so scary. And you know I think that a huge part of recovering from burnout is a deep understanding of yourself and what your needs are and what your triggers are, and you know, all the things. And it is like for a lot of people it feels like a privilege and a gift to be able to have time to do that. And it should just be normal practice, I think.

RPR: I've been thinking about how finally sharing my story was easier to do on Twitter because I don't really see those people. You don't "know" them. People in my life knew I was depressed and that I was on medical leave and those sorts of things, but I hadn't named everything that it was. When

I did, and I experienced this with a couple of people personally, they weren't ready to deal with themselves, so they couldn't deal with me. They could see themselves in what had happened to me, and they weren't ready to admit that it might be happening to them.

KL: Absolutely. Well burnout, it's a form of trauma. I think that on the other side of burnout, there's a feeling of gratitude and an acknowledgment of what really matters to people. One of the things that I appreciate about your story is that you did the work. I think there are people who just come in and out of burnout and they don't do the work, so they don't really understand what it is. And they don't know how to avoid it or how not to trigger it; they just have these cycles of burnout throughout their careers, some of which could last a long time, some of which could be more short-lived. But I think that that's the important work of this book, defining it for people so that they can be like, Oh so there's a name for this.

RPR: What are some of the other values that you think higher ed forces us into? What are some of the other things you see?

KL: Especially looking at the faculty role, one higher ed value is that you are loyal. I mean you're loyal to the institution that gives you tenure, and that to me has always been something I've questioned. If there's a mismatch between institutional culture and their own values, there can be a lot of issues that happen.

I think higher ed values history; I think higher ed values process. But also competition.

And I do think impostor syndrome. I don't know that we can call it a value, but it is definitely a hallmark of higher ed. Every academic woman I've worked with has imposter syndrome to some degree. It's almost trained into us in graduate school, where there's just no affirmation. You're constantly being questioned. There's definitely a value in there of causing insecurity and benefiting from other people's insecurity, which when you say it out loud is just awful. When you think about it that way . . . but that's really a lot of what's happening in higher education, it's really built on that.

For many people higher ed is a great fit for their personal values. But I also think what happens in graduate school is this breakdown of your own personal sense of what you are supposed to be doing. You need to get approval from your peers, your blind reviewers, your adviser, your department chair, or whatever board to get your promotion and tenure. There's always someone else deciding. Other people have to weigh in on your value and on your contributions. You aren't always the one who can say no, this is meaningful, and I don't need you to weigh in to know that.

Michelle Dionne Thompson

RPR: Tell us a little about your story, because you have a pretty unique background.

MDT: I first got my legal license and began working with people living with HIV in DC, then started working for a labor union. I loved the work, but I was working eighty hours a week for forty thousand dollars a year. I don't think there is a price that one should be paid to work eighty hours a week . . . that's just wrong.

I was totally burned out on law, and it was so fascinating I thought, I'm going to go do history. So I did the program, I graduated in 2012, and of course 2008 and the great recession happened, and you know, the job market. My committee wasn't supersupportive in terms of helping me find full-time faculty work, so I found myself adjuncting in New Jersey and at two colleges in Staten Island, so four courses—and I lived in Manhattan.

RPR: That's a lot to handle. How did you get into coaching?

MDT: I decided adjuncting was not going to work. At that point, I'd been part of a peer-counseling organization for almost twenty years, and I knew that I'd been able to build relationships with people; I'm wicked good at listening and wicked good at using tools to help turn people's lives around. I wanted to figure out how to use the skills and actually make money at it; I opened my email, and there was a scholarship to become a coach. I applied for the scholarship and got into the program, and I never looked back. I work with lawyers and academics; that's my professional background, and I see many similarities between the two industries and the ways in which women get set up. I bring that to my coaching.

RPR: What's important to you working with your clients?

MDT: With clients, we start with purpose. Especially during this pandemic, I've heard more people ask, why am I doing what I'm doing? Why am I writing? Why does this matter? Often my first question, before I hear a word about their field or project, is about their self-care. Tell me about how much sleep you get; what is your basic self-care routine? If you're not doing those basic things, you're actually leaving yourself very vulnerable. I also feel like the world of deductive reasoning in which we are trained to be academics has undermined our inner knowing about what we need and why we need it. I start by getting a read on how much people listen to their bodies and what they're trying to do.

RPR: How do you model that for clients? What does your self-care routine look like?

MDT: I've really been almost maniacal about making sure that I exercise every day. My sleep takes the first priority. I meditate and pray before I start things. So, I've done those three things to start my day with taking care of myself. Then I can move on to do other things, and I've been taking lots of quiet moments to listen to intuition. I've slowed down the pace of my day, and it turns out I can do more. Counterintuitive but so true.

I'm not here to get my clients working eighty hours a week. My job with clients has been to set them up with the professional habits they need so that they can ultimately put themselves and their families first. And then we work to learn how to set boundaries about what they're going to say yes and no to. I've watched them do this, and it's so rewarding.

RPR: Saying no can be so difficult, especially for junior faculty and women faculty more generally. Nos are so hard because you think, OK, well, this is going to get me in front of people, or if I don't do this, they'll never ask me again. My favorite story is from a junior faculty member I talked to who had only been in her position for maybe three years when I talked to her. She was asked to take on a big leadership role, one that is notoriously draining. She told them she would think about it for a few days, and then she came back two days later and said, "If I accept this role, I want to work under the current director for a year, and I want significant mentorship after that as well as X hours of admin support every week." They said yes, and she took the role on her own terms.

MDT: She thought to ask for this stuff. That's a big deal. Women don't often ask for things like that, whereas men will. We can say no, or we can set the terms on which we do this.

RPR: Changing gears a little, what advice would you give women who are already in burnout about building up their burnout resilience or things they can do to kind of prevent it from coming up again?

MDT: Stop.

I mean it. Just stop, if you think you're moving toward burnout. We can ignore the voice inside that's telling us we are doing too much, but if that voice is showing up, you need to heed it. It is time to stop and heed that voice. My first step is a stop to empty your calendar for the rest of the week. I'm not being sarcastic: empty your calendar for the rest of the week. The students will be glad to have a day off. Tell your colleagues you're really sick and you need time off. It's time to stop, which is going to be hard. But this is a time when you actually need to pay attention to what your body is telling you.

If you know your body, what does being tired tell you? Do you need to sleep? Sleep. Does that tiredness say you can't live on popcorn for the rest of your life? This is a time for you to actually take it up—take a moment to figure out how to get the food that nourishes you. Do you need to exercise? And if you're that tired, maybe you just need to do it. There's yoga—restorative yoga, not a lot of movement.

This is the time to stop and listen to your body. You can't listen to your mind; unplug, and listen to your body because your body will tell you everything you need to know.

Appendix 3

Additional Activities for Self-Exploration

This appendix provides additional opportunities for self-reflection via activities keyed to each of the book chapters. You'll find exercises that include written reflection, visual elements, and "tests" you can take. Complete them as you read through the corresponding chapters or on their own to continue building self-knowledge and strategies for addressing burnout.

Introduction

ABBREVIATED VERSION OF THE
MASLACH BURNOUT INVENTORY

As I discussed in the introduction, the Maslach Burnout Inventory is the most validated research instrument for documenting burnout. The website Mind-Tools offers a quick, free self-test version of the questionnaire, which I replicate here. You can use it to determine whether you want to complete the full inventory or seek support for further information.

On a scale of 1 to 5, with 1 being never and 5 being regularly, rate yourself on the following statements:

1. I feel run down and drained of physical or emotional energy.
2. I have negative thoughts about my job.
3. I am harder and less sympathetic with people than perhaps they deserve.
4. I am easily irritated by small problems, or by my coworkers and team.
5. I feel misunderstood or unappreciated by my coworkers.
6. I feel that I have no one to talk to.
7. I feel that I am achieving less than I should.
8. I feel under an unpleasant level of pressure to succeed.
9. I feel that I am not getting what I want out of my job.
10. I feel that I am in the wrong organization or the wrong profession.
11. I am frustrated with parts of my job.
12. I feel that organizational politics or bureaucracy frustrate my ability to do a good job.
13. I feel that there is more work to do than I practically have the ability to do.
14. I feel that I do not have time to do many of the things that are important to doing a good-quality job.
15. I find that I do not take the time to plan as much as I would like to.

If you answered mostly 1s, you are at little risk currently for burnout; mostly 2s, at some risk; mostly 3s, at risk, possibly in one of the three burnout dimensions more than the others; mostly 4s, at serious risk of burnout—consider seeking support; and mostly 5s, at severe risk—seek support as soon as possible.

Chapter 1

GIVES–DRAINS CONTINUUM

How does higher ed culture impact us collectively and individually? Draw a continuum with the words *Gives* and *Drains* at opposite ends. The center of the continuum is neutral. Give yourself a set time limit—three minutes at most—and think about which aspects of higher ed culture give you energy and which drain you. For example, things that give you energy might be seeing a student have an aha moment or working with your graduate students in the lab. Things that drain you might include enormous piles of grading or meetings with no agenda that could have been handled through email.

When your time is up, reflect on what you see. What are visible patterns? unexpected insights? reasons for concern? Are there certain features of higher ed that are most indicative of faculty burnout, either in others or in yourself?

Gives   Drains

$\longleftarrow\!\!\!\!\!\longrightarrow$

WOW, WONDERING, WORRIED

Take a few minutes to reflect on what you read in this chapter and spend some time journaling your responses to these questions: What wowed you? What are you wondering about? What worries you? Based on your reflection, what is one step you can take to address something you are wondering or worried about?

Chapter 2

PERSONAL INVENTORIES

I am the type of person who will do just about any magazine quiz or personality inventory I come across. I guess I just love tests. There are hundreds of validated and nonvalidated questionnaires out there, many of which you'll find on the *Psychology Today* website, that allow you to gain some additional self-knowledge that might be helpful, or at least amusing, as you explore your academic identity. Here are a few I like:

- Clance Imposter Phenomenon Scale (CIPS) for detecting imposter syndrome
- 16-Personalities version of the Big Five personality traits test
- Nate Silver version of the Big Five personality assessment
- Gretchen Rubin's Four Tendencies assessment
- Emotional Intelligence Test, using facial expressions to judge empathy
- Many more in Berkeley's Greater Good Science Center magazine

What did the quiz(zes) you took tell you about yourself broadly? What aspects do you agree or disagree with, and why? How might that extra self-knowledge help you think about your role and identity in higher education?

EMPATHY MAP

Offering ourselves compassion and empathy in the competitive, sometimes toxic culture of academia is crucial to mental health. Empathy maps are regularly used in design fields to better understand the user, customer, or client they hope to serve. Empathy maps can challenge common perceptions and force us to dig deeper to understand the stories we tell ourselves.

For this activity, create two separate empathy maps for yourself, one specific to work and one excluding everything work-related. Consider a typical day for you (if there is such a thing). While going about your work, what are you thinking, feeling, saying, and doing? What are you thinking, feeling, saying, and doing when you are not working?

Think	Feel
Say	Do

What did you learn about yourself from creating your empathy maps? What is surprising? What was revealed that you didn't know about yourself?

For an extra perspective, explain your empathy maps briefly to a trusted person and ask what they take away from your map.

THE PURPOSE TREE ACTIVITY

The following diagramming activity (adapted from Goncalves 2019) is an opportunity to refresh your self-knowledge by reconnecting to your purpose, values, and self. As I've mentioned before, these drawing activities can help us get out of our own heads and learn about ourselves in different ways. This particular version of the activity has been adapted from a team-building activity used by workplace teams to help team members reach a shared understanding of their work.

Consider the four areas of the "tree" that nourish and stabilize us:

1. The trunk represents your mission and vision. What is your vision of yourself and your activities when you look from a place of self-compassion rather than one of self-esteem?
2. The root system is composed of the values and beliefs that drive you, beyond what higher ed culture might demands. What grounds you? Who are you when you aren't "doing" higher ed? What keeps you strong?
3. Representing what we need to thrive in our environment are the natural elements that the tree needs to grow: sun, water, and soil. What gives you strength to grow? What happens when you don't have those things, and how can you address that absence?
4. And finally, the fruit the tree bears can signify accomplishments or self-knowledge gained when we pay attention to the trunk, the roots, and the natural elements of our environment. What manifests when you practice self-compassion? How do you talk to and treat yourself?

The Purpose Tree

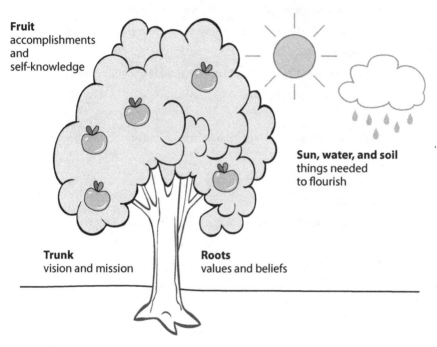

Fruit
accomplishments
and
self-knowledge

Sun, water, and soil
things needed
to flourish

Trunk
vision and mission

Roots
values and beliefs

The Purpose Tree Activity

What did you learn about yourself through this visualization exercise? How can
you use that knowledge to treat yourself, and therefore those you serve and
teach, better?

Chapter 4

ARE YOU EXPERIENCING EMOTIONAL EXHAUSTION?

Circle the statements that are true for you:

1. I smile less frequently than I used to, even in situations I typically
   would find funny.

2. My senses seem dulled, so food tastes flat, music doesn't move me, back rubs give me no pleasure, and I reach for black or gray clothes.

3. I can't sleep. Either I can't fall asleep or stay asleep or all I want to do is sleep.

4. Socializing is difficult. When I am with friends or family, I feel disconnected and have a hard time paying attention to what they say.

5. I am startled easily by voices, noises, or movement. I feel jumpy and jittery.

6. I am more irritable than I used to be, especially in lines, online, and on the phone.

7. My anxiety level is higher than usual, and crowds and traffic make me feel claustrophobic.

8. I cry more easily, particularly during movies, sad news reports, sentimental stories, and even shows with happy endings.

Any of these statements that are true for you can be signs of emotional exhaustion (see Witkin 2009). Think of ways to manage your stress and build self-compassion as you walk through these situations.

HEART, HEAD, HANDS

When you consider your faculty role in higher education, what mental pictures come to mind? What feelings come to the surface? What do you want to do, without thinking too much?

Heart, Head, Hands is a reflection activity aligned with acceptance commitment therapy that you can use to check in with yourself to discover insights about where you are right now. When I was ready to excavate the thoughts and feelings I had buried, I used this activity to look at different aspects of my professional life; for example, in one reflection, I used it to explore my relationship to higher education overall. I also used it to better understand my place at my institution and my teaching.

The activity is easy. Just choose a moment or topic and ask yourself what your mind says about your topic, what your heart is telling you, and then what you are doing or thinking of doing in relation to your topic. This activity is also an excellent reflection you can do as you move into your day in the morning or prepare for a restful evening.

Heart	
Head	
Hands	

Chapter 5

SOAR ANALYSIS, CONNECTION EDITION

Before digging into this chapter, take a moment to complete a SOAR analysis related to connection. Consider your strengths, opportunities, aspirations, and (desired) results in terms of connections to people, places, nature, arts, etc., whatever drives your inner sense of belonging.

Strengths	*Opportunities*	*Aspirations*	*Resources**

** Typically, the *R* here would represent results, but for our purposes, resources are a better reflection aspect.

Looking at your completed analysis, what are some ways you can act on your new knowledge and explore connecting?

THE SUCCESS PACK

Another way to think about a connection group or thinking partners is as what the coach and entrepreneur Charlie Gilkey (2020) calls the "Success Pack." This is the "group of people who are going to be instrumentally involved in helping you push your best-work project to done." In this simple exercise, you create a list of people who support you in different ways so that you have a go-to group for connection and bouncing ideas around. Here is a simple table to help you think about your own Success Pack:

Role	Name(s)	How can this person specifically help?
Guide		
Peer		
Supporter		
Beneficiary		

Once you've created your dream pack, reach out to those people for a conversation to solidify your thinking partnership and continue to build a relationship that is valuable for all of you.

WHAT IS, WHAT IF, WHAT WOWS, WHAT WORKS?

(Re)connecting with peers and colleagues, friends and family, even yourself and your values necessarily requires a certain level of self-excavation to get past the existing patterns. I had to do some hard work to understand why, and how, I had isolated myself during burnout and what I could do to connect more deeply at first with trusted family, friends, and peers and then more broadly. In a way, I had a design challenge. When approaching a design problem, you might explore four questions:

- What is?
- What if?
- What wows?
- What works?

Thinking about my burnout as a design problem some of the time helped me adapt reflection doings to pull myself out of rumination and catastrophizing and think productively and more realistically about the work I was doing to overcome burnout.

So, here's a more recent COVID-inspired example of how I might have used this structure to think more deeply about why I was isolating myself and how I might bring myself out of it:

- *What is?* Working from home is both great and hard. No commute, I have everything I need in the house, I can stay safe here, but I'm also not having much interaction with people other than my partner. No more conferences or even hallway chats. I'm lonely.

- *What if?* What if I resolved to talk with each of my colleagues one-on-one at least once every two weeks? What if I shared some stories and ideas with my Twitter followers to crowdsource ways to connect during the Zoom fatigue of the pandemic? What if I participated more consciously in some of the online groups I participate in? What if I just emailed people I think are cool to do coffee chats or interviews for the burnout book? What's the worst that could happen? They ignore me. Oh, well.

- *What wows?* Twitter is easy, so I can play with that. I really like the idea of just reaching out to people for coffee chats or interviews. It's definitely taking me out of my comfort zone. But I do want to connect more with other high-achieving women in and around academia; inviting them to be interviewed for the book or podcast could serve multiple purposes and help me connect more.

- *What worked?* Twitter wasn't as useful as I'd hoped. My following isn't big enough for that effort to work really. But almost everyone I invited for virtual coffee or an interview said yes! A couple of people just didn't respond, but that was fine. I had some great conversations with interesting women, even if it was out of my comfort zone to even ask. I feel more connected the more people I talk to in this way and am making some great networking connections as well. I'll keep doing these and use the book and podcast to encourage me.

How might you think about burnout, connection, and even burnout resilience as a design problem with this heuristic?

_____

_____

_____

Chapter 6

CHANGE TALK

If I could strike one sentence from every academic's brain, it would be "I should be writing." We use all manner of *should*, *need to*, and *must do* phrases in our everyday vocabulary, and each has some shame attached to it because you are calling yourself out for not doing whatever you *should* be doing—writing, grading, planning, did I say writing? Before burnout, if I wasn't using every single free minute to do something work-related, I berated myself for not working, for wasting time, for not doing whatever I was convinced I was supposed to be doing.

Changing that language from my inner critic was really hard work, but completely worth it. Try to rewire your own self-talk by replacing *I should* with

- I could
- I'd like to
- After I have rested, I can
- What's the worst that could happen if I don't . . . ?
- What's the best thing that could happen if I . . . ?

For example, my inner mentor says things like, "I would like to be writing, but my body is telling me I need to rest or move" and "My writing will still be there after I've gone to the barn to ride and replenish myself."

Another way to think about changing your self-talk is to add the words *so that I*. Whenever you have the thought "I should be writing," extend the thought to "I should be writing so that I. . . ." This additional phrase can help you get to the root of those *should*, *need to*, or *must* constructions and see where your values might be misaligned with your actions. You can add the phrase multiple times to get to the bottom of the thought. For example, "I should be writing" might become "I should be writing so that I can get this article finished . . . so that I can get it published . . . so that I can build up my CV . . . so that I can get promoted, etc." An inner-mentor version of this thought might look like this: "I could be writing so that I can share this research . . . so that my peers can use it in their courses . . . so that students ultimately benefit from this learning, etc."

What would your inner mentor say?

STARFISH REFLECTION

Thinking about how you spend your time and energy across all aspects of your life, use this pattern to get real with yourself about how you would actually like to be using your time and energy to create more balance.

Starfish Reflection

Appendix 4

Reflecting on Your Relationship with Work and Burnout

Reflection questions and activities throughout the book offer opportunities to explore your thoughts and feelings about work and burnout. But if you are new to such reflection or just beginning to explore your relationship to work, here are some guided questions you might consider. (You might also want to take the abbreviated Maslach Burnout Inventory in appendix 3 or the complete version available from mindgarden.com.)

What attracted you to higher education?

What were you most passionate about when you began your career in higher ed?

What motivates you most to fulfill your purpose—in general and in higher ed?

When do you feel your best at work?

What values and meaningful goals do you have for your academic career? Do you feel as if you are honoring those values and goals currently? Why, or why not?

What's the most meaningful reason that you do your work?

Indicators of workplace well-being include job satisfaction, quitting intentions, job involvement, engagement, organizational commitment, and organizational citizenship behaviors. How do you relate to each of these elements? How are you experiencing workplace well-being?

Is there a specific time you can identify when your passion waned? What happened? How did you rebound, or why didn't you rebound?

What aspects of your work, if any, do you dread? Why? What underlies that dread? What would happen if you stopped doing that thing?

How often do you feel exhausted (physically, emotionally, intellectually, etc.) or cynical about your work? What are you doing when you feel this way?

If you could change anything about your current context, what would it be, and why? If those things magically changed one night, how would you know it the next day? How would you feel? What would you do?

What is most challenging for you when you think about your future in higher education?

References

Ahmad, A. S. 2020. A survival guide for black, indigenous, and other women of color in academe. *Chronicle of Higher Education,* 6 July. https://www.chronicle.com/article/a-survival-guide-for-black-indigenous-and-other-women-of-color-in-academe.

Alarcon, G., K. J. Eschleman, and N. A. Bowling. 2009. Relationships between personality variables and burnout: A meta-analysis. *Work & Stress* 23 (3): 244–63.

Alvesson, M. 2009. At-home ethnography: Struggling with closeness and closure. In (eds.), *Organizational Ethnography,* ed. S. Ybema, D. Yanow, H. Wels, and F. Kamsteeg, 156–74. London: Sage.

Ambrose, S. A., M. W. Bridges, M. DiPietro, M. C. Lovett, and M. K. Norman. 2010. *How Learning Works: Seven Research-Based Principles for Smart Teaching.* San Francisco: Jossey-Bass.

Aronowitz, S. 2000. *The Knowledge Factory: Dismantling the Corporate University and Creating True Higher Learning.* Boston: Beacon Press.

Austin, A. E. 2002. Preparing the next generation of faculty: Graduate school as socialization to the academic career. *Journal of Higher Education* 73 (1): 94–122.

Bahn, K. 2014. Faking it: Women, academia, and impostor syndrome. Chronicle Vitae, 27 March. https://www.google.com/url?sa=t&rct=j&q=&esrc=s&source=web&cd=&ved=2ahUKEwjWtaKZmdX1AhXIct8KHfl_BGQQFnoECAQQAQ&url=https%3A%2F%2Fcommunity.csusm.edu%2Fmod%2Fresource%2Fview.php%3Fid%3D43723&usg=AOvVaw3MyAAPC3hYb7EDQ2ZPr-e4.

Bain, K. 2004. *What the Best College Teachers Do.* Cambridge, MA: Harvard University Press.

Baker, K. J. 2017. *Grace Period: A Memoir in Pieces*. Chapel Hill, NC: Blue Crow Books.

Baldwin, R. 1990. Faculty vitality beyond the research university: Extending a contextual concept. *Journal of Higher Education* 61 (2): 160–80.

Baldwin, R. G., D. DeZhure, A. Shaw, and K. Moretto. 2008. Mapping the terrain of mid career faculty at a research university: Implications for faculty and academic leaders. *Change* 50 (5): 46–55.

Baldwin, R. G., C. J. Lunceford, and K. E. Vanderlinden. 2005. Faculty in the middle years: Illuminating an overlooked phase of academic life. *Review of Higher Education* 29 (1): 97–118.

Billot, J. 2010. The imagined and the real: Identifying the tensions for academic identity. *Higher Education Research & Development* 29 (6): 709–21.

Blix, A., R. J. Cruise, B. N. Mitchell, and G. G. Blix. 1994. Occupational stress among university teachers. *Educational Research* 36 (2): 157–69.

Bothello, J., and T. J. Roulet. 2019. The imposter syndrome, or the mis-representation of self in academic life. *Journal of Management Studies* 56 (4): 854–61.

Bousquet, Marc. 2008. *How the University Works: Higher Education and the Low-Wage Nation*. Vol. 3. New York: New York University Press.

Brems, C., M. R. Baldwin, L. Davis, and L. Namyniuk. 1994. The imposter syndrome as related to teaching evaluations and advising relationships of university faculty members. *Journal of Higher Education* 65 (2): 183–93.

Brown, B. 2012. *Daring Greatly: How the Courage to Be Vulnerable Transforms the Way We Live, Love, Parent, and Lead*. New York: Avery.

———. 2017. *Rising Strong: How the Ability to Rest Transforms the Way We Live, Love, Parent, and Lead*. New York: Random House.

Cardel, M. I., N. Dean, and D. Montoya-Williams. 2020. Preventing a secondary epidemic of lost early career scientists: Effects of COVID-19 pandemic on women with children. *Annuals of the American Thoracic Society* 17 (11): 1366–70.

Cardel, M. I., E. Dhurandhar, C. Yarar-Fisher, M. Foster, B. Hidalgo, L. A. McClure, S. Pagoto, et al. 2020. Turning chutes into ladders for women faculty: A review and roadmap for equity in academia. *Journal of Women's Health* 29 (5): 721–33.

Cavanagh, S. R. 2019. *Hivemind: The New Science of Tribalism in Our Divided World*. New York: Grand Central.

———. 2021. Interviewed by Rebecca Pope-Ruark. *The agile academic* (audio podcast), 2 March. https://theagileacademic.buzzsprout.com/1637707/8039299-sarah-rose -cavanagh-on-writing-self-care-and-connection.

Clance, P. R., and S. Imes. 1978. The imposter phenomenon in high achieving women: Dynamics and therapeutic intervention. *Psychotherapy Theory, Research and Practice* 15 (3): 1–8.

Clegg, S. 2008. Academic identities under threat? *British Educational Journal* 34 (3): 329–45.

Cokley, K., L. Smith, D. Bernard, A. Hurst, S. Jackson, S. Stone, O. Awosogba, C. Saucer, M. Bailey, and D. Roberts. 2017. Impostor feelings as a moderator and mediator of the relationship between perceived discrimination and mental health among racial/ethnic minority college students. *Journal of Counseling Psychology* 64 (2): 141–54.

Cook-Sather, A., C. Bovill, and P. Felten. 2014. *Engaging Students as Partners in Learning and Teaching: A Guide for Faculty.* San Francisco: Jossey-Bass.

Corbera, E., I. Anguelovski, J. Honey-Rosés, and I. Ruiz-Mallén. 2020. Academia in the time of COVID-19: Towards an ethics of care. *Planning Theory & Practice* 21 (2): 191–99.

Costa, K. 2021. Interview by Rebecca Pope-Ruark. *The agile academic* (audio podcast), 9 February. https://theagileacademic.buzzsprout.com/1637707/7445434-karen -costa-on-online-education-and-the-higher-in-higher-ed.

Cox, M. D., and L. Richlin. 2004. *Building Faculty Learning Communities.* New Directions for Teaching and Learning, no. 97. San Francisco: Jossey-Bass.

Dancy, T. E., and M. C. Brown. 2011. The mentoring and induction of educators of color: Addressing the impostor syndrome in academe. *Journal of School Leadership* 21 (4): 607–34.

Dancy, T. E., and J. M. Gaetane. 2014. Faculty of color in higher education: Exploring the intersections of identity, impostorship, and internalized racism. *Mentoring & Tutoring: Partnership in Learning* 22 (4): 354–72.

DeFilippo, A. M., and D. E. Giles Jr. 2015. Mid-career faculty and high levels of community engagement: Intentional reshaping of meaningful careers. *International Journal of Research on Service-Learning and Community Engagement* 3 (1).

Deligkaris, P., E. Panagopoulou, A. J. Montgomery, and E. Masoura. 2014. Job burnout and cognitive functioning: A systematic review. *Work & Stress* 28 (4): 107–23.

Demerouti, E., and A. B. Bakker. 2008. The Oldenburg Burnout Inventory: A good alternative to measure burnout and engagement. In *Handbook of Stress and Burnout in Health Care*, ed. J. R. B. Halbesleben, 65–78. New York: Nova Science.

Dodes, J. 2019. Why do achievements leave me feeling empty? *Unhappy Achievers* (blog), *Psychology Today*, 8 April. https://www.psychologytoday.com/us/blog /unhappy-achievers/201904/why-do-achievements-leave-me-feeling-empty.

Dodes, L. 2017. Are you an unhappy achiever? *The Heart of Addiction* (blog), *Psychology Today*, 31 August. https://www.psychologytoday.com/us/blog/the-heart-addiction/201708/are-you-unhappy-achiever.

Dweck, C. 2016. What having a "growth mindset" actually means. *Harvard Business Review* 13:213–26.

Erikson, E. H. 1969. *Ghandi's Truth*. Magnolia, MA: Peter Smith.

Esfahani Smith, E. 2017. *The Power of Meaning: Crafting a Life that Matters*. New York: Crown.

Fass, C. 2021. Interviewed by Rebecca Pope-Ruark. *The agile academic* (audio podcast), 12 July. https://theagileacademic.buzzsprout.com/1637707/8851972-caitlin-faas-on-coaching-self-care-and-self-knowledge.

Fink, L. D. 2013. *Creating Significant Learning Experiences: An Integrated Approach to Designing College Courses*. San Francisco: Jossey-Bass.

Flaherty, C. 2020a. Babar in the room. *Inside Higher Ed*, 11 August. https://www.insidehighered.com/news/2020/08/11/faculty-parents-are-once-again-being-asked-perform-miracle.

———. 2020b. Burning out. *Inside Higher Ed*, 14 September. https://www.insidehighered.com/news/2020/09/14/faculty-members-struggle-burnout.

———. 2020c. Faculty pandemic stress is now chronic. *Inside Higher Ed*, 19 November. https://www.insidehighered.com/news/2020/11/19/faculty-pandemic-stress-now-chronic.

Ford, J., N. Harding, and M. Learmonth. 2010. Who is it that would make business schools more critical? *Critical Reflections on Critical Management Studies* 23:31–34.

Frankl, V. E. 1962. Psychiatry and man's quest for meaning. *Journal of Religion and Health* 1 (2): 93–103.

French, S., A. Patriarca, and J. Veltsos. 2021. Interview by Rebecca Pope-Ruark. *The agile academic* (audio podcast), 23 January. https://theagileacademic.buzzsprout.com/1637707/7442926-backchanneling-for-women-in-higher-ed.

Gee, J. P. 2001. Chapter 3: Identity as an analytic lens for research in education. *Review of Research in Education* 25 (1): 99–125.

Ghorpade, J., J. Lackritz, and G. Singh. 2007. Burnout and personality: Evidence from academia. *Journal of Career Assessment* 15 (2): 240–56.

Gilkey, C. 2020. How success packs push your project to done. Productive Flourishing, 13 March. https://www.productiveflourishing.com/success-packs/.

Giroux, H. 2002. Neoliberalism, corporate culture, and the promise of higher education: The university as a democratic public sphere. *Harvard Educational Review* 72 (4): 425–64.

———. 2003. Selling out higher education. *Policy Futures in Education* 1 (1): 179–200.

Glisson, C. 2015. The role of organizational culture and climate in innovation and effectiveness. *Human Service Organizations, Management, Leadership & Governance* 39 (4): 245–50.

Goncalves, L. 2019. Using the high-performance tree in your Agile retrospectives. Reinventing Organizations, 14 September. https://luis-goncalves.com/high -performance-tree-retrospectives/.

González-Romá, V., W. B. Schaufeli, A. B. Bakker, and S. Lloret. 2006. Burnout and work engagement: Independent factors or opposite poles? *Journal of Vocational Behavior* 68:165–74.

Gooler, D. D. 1991. *Professorial Vitality: A Critical Issue in Higher Education*. DeKalb, IL: LEPS Press.

Gorski, P. C. 2015. Relieving burnout and the "martyr syndrome" among social justice education activists: The implications and effects of mindfulness. *Urban Review* 47 (4): 696–716.

Gravois, J. 2007. You're not fooling anyone. *Chronicle of Higher Education*, 9 November. https://www.chronicle.com/article/youre-not-fooling-anyone/.

Green, A. 2016. Seven dimensions of wellness: A holistic approach to health. *Alive*, 18 January, 15–23.

Gruber, J., J. J. Van Bavel, W. A. Cunningham, L. H. Somerville, and N. A. Lewis Jr. 2020. Academia needs a reality check: Life is not back to normal. *Science*, 28 August. https://www.science.org/content/article/academia-needs-reality-check -life-not-back-normal.

Hall, D. T. 1986. Breaking career routines: Midcareer choice and identity development. In *Career Development in Organizations*, ed. D. T. Hall, 120–59. San Francisco: Jossey-Bass.

Hall, E. 2018. *Aristotle's Way: How Ancient Wisdom Can Change Your Life*. New York: Penguin.

Hallett, K. 2018. *Be Awesome! Banish Burnout: Create Motivation from the Inside Out*. Self-published.

———. 2020. You're not an imposter; You're human. YouTube. https://www.youtube.com /watch?v=WMYiXTothqM&t=177s.

Hanson, R., with F. Hanson. 2018. *Resilient: How to Grow an Unshakable Core of Calm, Strength, and Happiness.* New York: Harmony Books.

Hari, J. 2018. *Lost Connections: Why We're Depressed and How to Find Hope.* New York: Bloomsbury.

Harley, S. 2002. The impact of research selectivity on academic work and identity in UK universities. *Studies in Higher Education* 27:159–205.

Harnish, R. J., and H. R. Bridges. 2011. Effect of syllabus tone: Students' perceptions of instructor and course. *Social Psychology of Education: An International Journal* 14 (3): 319–30.

Harrison, B. J. 1999. Are you destined to burnout out? *Fund Raising Management* 30 (3): 25–27.

Harvey, J. C., and C. Katz. 1985. *If I'm So Successful, Why Do I Feel Like a Fake? The Impostor Phenomenon.* New York: St. Martin's Press.

Headlee, C. 2020. *Do Nothing: How to Break Away from Overworking, Overdoing, and Underliving.* New York: Harmony.

Hearn, J. 2008. Feeling out of place? Toward the transnationalization on emotions. In *The Emotional Organization: Passions and Power,* 184–201. London: Blackwell.

Henry, T. 2013. *Die Empty: Unleash Your Best Work Every Day.* New York: Portfolio Press.

Hubbard, G. T., and S. S. Atkins. 1995. The professor as a person: The role of faculty well-being in faculty development. *Innovative Higher Education* 20 (2): 117–28.

Hubbard, G. T., S. S. Atkins, and K. T. Brinko. 1998. Holistic faculty development: Supporting personal, professional, and organizational well-being. *To Improve the Academy* 17 (1): 35–49.

Hutchins, H. M., and H. Rainbolt. 2017. What triggers imposter phenomenon among academic faculty? A critical incident study exploring antecedents, coping, and development opportunities. *Human Resource Development International* 20 (3): 194–214.

Jaffe, S. 2021. *Work Won't Love You Back: How Devotion to Our Jobs Keeps Us Exploited, Exhausted, and Alone.* New York: Bold Type Books.

Jamal, J., and V. V. Baba. 2001. Type-A behavior, job performance, and well-being in college teachers. *International Journal of Stress Management* 8 (3): 231–40.

Jaremka, L M., J. M. Ackerman, B. Gawronski, N. O. Rule, K. Sweeny, L. R. Tropp, M. A. Metz, L. Molina, W. S. Ryan, and S. B. Vick. 2020. Common academic experiences no one talks about: Repeated rejection, impostor syndrome, and burnout. *Perspectives on Psychological Science* 15 (3): 519–43.

Jawitz, J. 2009. Academic identities and communities of practice in a professional discipline. *Teaching in Higher Education* 14 (3): 241–51.

Jessop, Bob. 2018. On academic capitalism. *Critical Policy Studies* 12 (1): 104–9.

Kalivoda, P., G. Rogers Sorrell, and R. D. Simpson. 1994. Nurturing faculty vitality by matching institutional interventions with career-stage needs. *Innovative Higher Education* 18 (4): 255–72.

Kaplan, K. 2009. Unmasking the impostor. *Nature* 459:668–69.

Karpiak, I. E. 1997. University professors at mid-life: Being a part of . . . but feeling apart. *To Improve the Academy* 16:21–40.

Kasper, J. 2013. An academic with imposter syndrome. *Chronicle of Higher Education*, 2 April. https://www.chronicle.com/article/an-academic-with-impostor-syndrome/.

Keenan, C. 2016. Reclaiming authenticity. *Inside Higher Ed*, 20 October. https://www.insidehighered.com/advice/2016/10/20/women-academic-leaders-and-impostor-syndrome-essay.

Knights, D., and C. A. Clarke. 2014. It's a bittersweet symphony, this life: Fragile academic selves and insecure identities at work. *Organization Studies* 35 (3): 335–57.

Koenig, R. 2019. "Academic Capitalism" is reshaping faculty life. What does that mean? EdSurge, 25 November. https://www.edsurge.com/news/2019-11-25-academic-capitalism-is-reshaping-faculty-life-what-does-that-mean.

Kolomitro, K., N. Kenny, and S. Le-May Sheffield. 2020. A call to action: Exploring and responding to educational developers' workplace burnout and well-being in higher education. *International Journal for Academic Development* 25 (1): 5–18.

Kramer, J. 2020. The virus moved female faculty to the brink. Will universities help? *New York Times*, 6 October. https://www.nytimes.com/2020/10/06/science/covid-universities-women.html.

Kristensen, T. S., M. Borritz, E. Villadsen, and K. B. Christensen. 2005. The Copenhagen Burnout Inventory: A new tool for the assessment of burnout. *Work & Stress* 19 (3): 192–207.

Krukowski, R. A., R. Jagsi, and M. I. Cardel. 2021. Academic productivity differences by gender and child age in science, technology, engineering, mathematics, and medicine faculty during the COVID-19 pandemic. *Journal of Women's Health* 30 (3): 341–47.

Lackritz, J. R. 2004. Exploring burnout among university faculty: Incidence, performance, and demographic issues. *Teaching and Teacher Education* 20:713–29.

L'Engle, M. 1963. *A Wrinkle in Time*. New York: Square Fish.

Lieff, S., L. Baker, B. Mori, E. Egan-Lee, K. Chin, and S. Reeves. 2012. Who am I? Key influences on the formation of academic identity within a faculty development program. *Medical Teacher* 34 (3): e208–e215.

Lionni, L. 1967. *Frederick*. New York: Pantheon.

Loonstra, B., A. Brouwres, and W. Tomic. 2009. Feelings of existential fulfillment and burnout among secondary school teachers. *Teaching and Teacher Education* 25:752–57.

Lumpkin, A. 2014. The role of organizational culture on and career stages of faculty. *Educational Forum* 78 (2): 196–205.

Machell, D. F. 1988. A discourse on professorial melancholia. *Community Review* 9 (1–2): 41–50.

Malesic, J. 2016. The 40-year-old burnout. *Chronicle of Higher Education*, 5 October. https://www.chronicle.com/article/the-40-year-old-burnout/.

Malisch, J. L., B. N. Harris, S. M. Sherrer, K. A. Lewis, S. L. Shepherd, P. C. McCarthy, J. L. Spott, et al. 2020. Opinion: In the wake of COVID-19, academia needs new solutions to ensure gender equity. *Proceedings of the National Academy of Sciences* 117 (27): 15378–81.

Maslach, C., S. E. Jackson, and M. P. Leiter. 1996. *Maslach Burnout Inventory Manual*. 3rd ed. Palo Alto, CA: Consulting Psychologists Press.

Maslach, C., and M. Leiter. 2015. It's time to take action on burnout. *Burnout Research* 2 (1): iv–v.

Maslach, C., W. B. Schaufeli, and M. P. Leiter. 2001. Job burnout. *Annual Review of Psychology* 52:397–422.

Mayo Clinic. 2021. Job burnout: How to spot it and take action. https://www.mayoclinic.org/healthy-lifestyle/adult-health/in-depth/burnout/art-20046642.

McMillan, B. 2016. Think like an impostor, and you'll go far in academia. *Times Higher Education*, 18 April. https://www.timeshighereducation.com/blog/think-impostor-and-youll-go-far-academia.

McMurtrie, B. 2020. The pandemic is dragging on: Professors are burning out. *Chronicle of Higher Education*, 5 November. https://www.chronicle.com/article/the-pandemic-is-dragging-on-professors-are-burning-out.

MindTools. n.d. Burnout self-test: Checking yourself for burnout. https://www.mindtools.com/pages/article/newTCS_08.htm.

Nagoski, E., and A. Nagoski. 2019. *Burnout: The Secret to Unlocking the Stress Cycle*. New York: Ballantine Books.

National Wellness Institute. 2019. Six dimensions of wellness model. https://www
.nationalwellness.org/page/AboutWellness.

Neff, K. D., K. L. Kirkpatrick, and S. S. Rude. 2007. Self-compassion and adaptive
psychological functioning. *Journal of Research in Personality* 41 (1): 139–54.

Neff, K. D., and R. Vonk. 2009. Self-compassion versus global self-esteem: Two different
ways of relating to oneself. *Journal of Personality* 77 (1): 23–50.

Odell, J. 2019. *How to Do Nothing: Resisting the Attention Economy.* New York: Melville
House.

O'Meara, K., A. L. Terosky, and A. Neumann. 2008. *Faculty Careers and Work Lives: A
Professional Growth Perspective.* ASHE Higher Education Report. Hoboken, NJ:
Wiley.

O'Meara, R. 2017. *Pause: Harnessing the Life-Changing Power of Giving Yourself a
Break.* New York: Tarcher Perigee.

O'Reilley, M. R. 2005. *The Garden at Night: Burnout and Breakdown in the Teaching
Life.* Portsmouth, NH: Heinneman.

Oxenford, C. B., and S. L. Kublenschmidt. 2011. Working effectively with psychologi-
cally impaired faculty. *To Improve the Academy* 30 (1): 186–201.

Padilla, A. M. 1994. Ethnic minority scholars, research, and mentoring: Current and
future issues. *Educational Researcher* 23 (4): 24–27.

Padilla, M. A., and J. N. Thompson. 2016. Burning out faculty at doctoral research
universities. *Stress and Health* 32 (5): 551–58.

Pang, A. S. 2018. *Rest: Why You Get More Done When You Work Less.* New York: Basic
Books.

Park, T. 2011. Academic capitalism and its impact on the American professoriate.
Journal of the Professoriate 6 (1): 84–96.

Pedersen, D. E., and K. L. Minnotte. 2017. Workplace climate and STEM faculty
women's job burnout. *Journal of Feminist Family Therapy* 29 (1–2): 45–65.

Pines, A. M. 1993. Burnout. In *Handbook of Stress: Theoretical and Clinical Aspects*, ed.
L. Goldberger and S. Breznitz, 386–402. 2nd ed. New York: Free Press.

Readings, B. 1996. *The University in Ruins.* Cambridge, MA: Harvard University Press.

Reis, D., D. Xanthopoulou, and I. Tsaousis. 2015. Measuring job and academic burnout
with the Oldenburg Burnout Inventory (OLBI): Factorial invariance across
samples and countries. *Burnout Research* 2 (1): 8–18.

Rendón, L. I. 2009. *Sentipensante (sensing/thinking) Pedagogy: Educating for
Wholeness, Social Justice and Liberation.* Sterling, VA: Stylus.

Reybold, L. E. 2003. Pathways to the professorate: The development of faculty identity in education. *Innovative Higher Education* 27 (4): 235–52.

Richards, R., K. Andrew, and C. Levesque-Bristol. 2016. Assisting in the management of faculty role stress: Recommendations for faculty developers. *Journal of Faculty Development* 30 (1): 7–14.

Rippeyoung, P. 2012. The imposter syndrome, or, as my mother told me: "Just because everyone else is an asshole, it doesn't make you a fraud." (A guest post). The Professor Is In, 11 December. https://theprofessorisin.com/2012/12/11 /the-imposter-syndrome-or-as-my-mother-told-me-just-because-everyone-else -is-an-asshole-it-doesnt-make-you-a-fraud-a-guest-post/.

Roesner, R.W., E. Skinner, J. Beers, and P. A. Jennings. 2012. Mindfulness training and teachers' professional development: An emerging area of research and practice. *Child Development Perspectives* 6 (2): 167–73.

Rook, K. S. 2015. Social networks in later life: Weighing positive and negative effects on health and well-being. *Current Directions in Psychological Science* 24 (1): 45–51.

Ross, C. 2015. Teaching renewal for midcareer faculty: Attending to the whole person. *To Improve the Academy* 34 (1–2): 270–89.

Rudenga, K. J., and E. O. Gravett. 2019. Impostor phenomenon in educational developers. *To Improve the Academy* 38 (1): 1–17.

———. 2021. Impostor phenomenon in educational developers: Consequences and coping strategies. *To Improve the Academy* 39 (2). https://quod.lib.umich.edu/t/tia /17063888.0039.201?view=text;rgn=main.

Sabagh, Z., N. C. Hall, and A. Saroyan. 2018. Antecedents, correlates and consequences of faculty burnout. *Educational Research* 60 (2): 131–56.

Schaufeli, W. B., and A. B. Bakker. 2001. Work and well-being: Towards a positive approach in Occupational Health Psychology. *Gedrag & Organisatie* 14:229–53.

———. 2004. Job demands, job resources and their relationship with burnout and engagement: A multi-sample study. *Journal of Organizational Behavior* 25:293–315.

Schubert-Irastorza, C., and D. L. Fabry. 2014. Job satisfaction, burnout and work engagement in higher education: A survey of research and best practices. *Journal of Research in Innovative Teaching* 7 (1): 37–50.

Schwartz, B., and K. Sharpe. 2010. *Practical Wisdom: The Right Way to Do the Right Thing.* New York: Riverhead Books.

Segal, K. A. 2020. Exploration of Integrative Mental Health Practitioner Wellness: An Interpretive Phenomenological Analysis. PhD diss., Saybrook University.

Stupnisky, R. H., N. C. Hall, and R. Pekrun. 2019a. The emotions of pre-tenure faculty: Implications for teaching and research success. *Review of Higher Education* 42 (4): 1489–1526.

——. 2019b. Faculty enjoyment, anxiety, and boredom for teaching and research: Instrument development and testing predictors of success. *Studies in Higher Education* 44 (10): 1712–22.

Tedeschi, R. G., and L. G. Calhoun. 2004) Posttraumatic growth: Conceptual foundations and empirical evidence. *Psychological Inquiry* 15 (1): 1–18.

Teven, J. J. 2007. Teacher temperament: Correlates with teacher caring, burnout, and organizational outcomes. *Communication Education* 56 (3): 382–400.

Thomason, T. C. 2012. A week in the life of a university professor: Issues of stress, workload, and wellness. *Counseling & Wellness: A Professional Counseling Journal* 3:23–36.

Van Aken, E. M., D. J. Monetta, and D. S. Sink. 1994. Affinity groups: The missing link in employee involvement. *Organizational Dynamics* 22 (4): 38–54.

Wang, H., N. C. Hall, and S. Rahimi. 2015. Self-efficacy and causal attributions in teachers: Effects on burnout, job satisfaction, illness, and quitting intentions. *Teaching and Teacher Education* 47:120–30.

Watts, A. 1977. *Psychotherapy East and West.* Harmondsworth, UK: Penguin.

Watts, J., and N. Robertson. 2011. Burnout in university teaching staff: A systematic literature review. *Educational Research* 53 (1): 33–50.

Weimer, M. 2013. *Learner-Centered Teaching: Five Key Changes to Practice.* San Francisco: Jossey-Bass.

Westerman, J. W., B. G. Whitaker, J. Z. Bergman, S. M. Bergman, and J. P. Daly. 2016. Faculty narcissism and student outcomes in business higher education: A student-faculty fit analysis. *International Journal of Management Education* 14 (2): 63–73.

Whitman, M. V., and K. K. Shanine. 2012. Revisiting the imposter phenomenon: How individuals cope with feelings of being in over their head. *Research in Occupational Stress* 10:177–212.

Winter, R. 2009. Academic manager or managed academic? Academic identity schisms in higher education. *Journal of Higher Education Policy and Management* 31 (2): 121–31.

Witkin, G. 2019. 8 questions to check if you are emotionally exhausted. *Psychology Today*, 21 May. https://www.psychologytoday.com/us/blog/the-chronicles-infertility/201905/8-questions-check-if-youre-emotionally-exhausted.

World Health Organization (WHO). 2019. Burnout an "occupational phenomenon": International Classification of Diseases. 28 May. https://www.who.int/news/item

/28-05-2019-burn-out-an-occupational-phenomenon-international-classification-of
-diseases.

Young, C. 2020. Pandemic exacerbates already high levels of stress among women faculty. *Ms. Magazine*, 7 October. https://msmagazine.com/2020/10/07/coronavirus-covid
-19-mental-health-stress-women-faculty-teachers-colleges-universities/.

Zorn, D. 2005. Academic culture feeds the imposter phenomenon. *Academic Leader* 21 (8): 1–2.

Index

Big Five personality assessment, 213
Billot, J., 59
Bird by Bird (Lamott), 72
book discussions, 201
boundaries, 171–72, 174–80, 208
Brinko, Kate, 201
Brouwres, Andre, 90
Brown, Brené: on boundaries, 175, 176; on
    burnout, 1; on compassion, 110, 130; on ego,
    125; on emotional accessibility, 113; on
    narcissism, 70; on perfectionism, 87; on
    vulnerability, 68
Buddhism, 127
bullying and harassment, 10, 197; in academic
    cultures, 39–43; antibullying efforts, 99;
    masked as mentoring and support, 43; sexual
    harassment, 40–41
burnout: causes of, 8–9; COVID-19 pandemic and,
    14–16; culture of higher education and, 16–17;
    cycles of, 206; defined, 7–9; in higher educa-
    tion, 10–14; physical symptoms of, 9, 168–69,
    172–73; recovery from, 87–88, 124–33, 149,
    184–86, 205; reflection on, 23–24, 222–24;
    retreat to combat, 202; as trauma, 206. *See also*
    specific symptoms
burnout-resilience workshops, 28–29
busyness, 7, 16, 170–71, 174

Calarico, Jessica, 15
calling versus job, 19, 27, 31, 85–86
capitalism, 48–52, 178–80. *See also* academic
    capitalism
career reflection exercise, 193–95
catastrophizing, 4, 126, 129
Cavanagh, Sarah Rose, 138, 157
childcare, 12, 15, 165
Chronicle of Higher Education (journal), 15, 46
chronic stress, 7–9, 75, 91, 168–69, 172–73
Clance Imposter Phenomenon Scale (CIPS), 213
Clarke, Caroline, 41, 43, 59–60
coaching as profession, 20, 188. *See also specific*
    coaches by name
cognitive distortions, 126, 129
collaborative environment, 37–38
comfort zones, 185–86
communities of practice, 199–200
community. *See* connection
compassion, 21, 105–34; burnout resilience and,
    19; empathy maps and, 213; exercise and ac-
    tivities for, 111–12, 215–17; exhaustion and,
    112–16; gaslighting and depersonalizing,
    117–26; inner critic versus inner mentor,
    129; loss of, 75; reflection on, 107, 111–12,
    116–17, 134; self-compassion and recovery,
    124–33; significance of, 107–12
compassion fatigue, 112–16, 122–23
competition: connection and, 139–40; as core
    value, 86; culture and, 42–45, 60, 85–86, 117,

206; within departments, 37–38, 139; nemesis
    as, 42; for outside funding, 31–32; perfection-
    ism and, 73; too few jobs for graduate pool, 44
concentration, loss of, 1–3, 8
confidentiality, 120
confusion and misalignment, 89, 117, 203–4, 206
connection, 21, 135–59; burnout resilience and,
    19; community-building within institutions,
    144–50; competition and, 139–40; exercises
    and activities for, 158, 217–20; imposter syn-
    drome and, 67–68; inside outside observers
    (partners of academics) and, 140–43; outside
    academia, 156–59; outside institutions, 150–
    56; overview, 138–39; reflection on, 137–38,
    143; SOAR analysis and, 217
contentment, 164–65
contingent faculty. *See* adjunct and non-tenure-
    track (NTT) faculty
coping skills: compassion fatigue and, 122;
    depersonalization and, 75, 122; exhaustion
    and, 114, 134; for imposter syndrome, 65,
    67–68, 78; institutional resources and, 120;
    meaningful purpose, pursuit of, 84;
    perfectionism and, 70, 74; self-compassion
    and, 125
Corbera, Esteve, 47
corporatization of higher education, 31–32,
    49–50
Costa, Karen, 65
Course Hero, 14
COVID-19 pandemic: burnout and, 14–16; cul-
    ture of higher education and, 47; hobbies not
    possible during, 183; minorities and, 15, 165;
    online courses and, 54–55, 123; overworking
    and, 165; What Is, What If, What Wows,
    What Works? exercise and, 219
Creagan, Edward, 197
cross-fertilization, 184–86
crying, 112–13, 116, 216
culture of higher education, 20–21, 25–52;
    boundaries and, 174–80; burnout and, 16–17;
    busyness and, 170–71, 174; calling out, 38–42;
    competition and, 42–45, 60, 85–86, 117; core
    values versus, 117; employment and, 30–38;
    exercises and activities for, 211–12; gender
    roles and, 118, 120; mental health issues and,
    115–16; navigating, 46–48; prevalence of
    burnout and, 28–30; reflection on, 28, 48;
    resisting, 48–52; social and administrative
    support, 139; value system and, 203–7
cynicism, 9, 14, 55, 93

Dancy, T. Elon, II, 69
data sharing, 37
depersonalization: burnout and, 1, 3, 9, 13, 75, 93;
    compassion and, 117–26; compassion fatigue
    and, 122–23; symptoms of, 113
depression, 8–9, 54, 99, 115, 126, 139

race. *See* minorities
Rainbolt, Hilary, 67, 70, 120, 125, 150
recognition and awards. *See* external validation
recovery from burnout, 87–88, 124–33, 149, 184–86, 205, 209
reflection: on academic identity, 55–56; on balance, 162–63, 187; on burnout, 23–24, 222–24; on career and legacy, 193–95; on compassion, 107, 111–12, 116–17, 134; on connection, 137–38, 143; on culture, 28, 48; on purpose, 82, 84, 90, 103, 194; self-reflection, 202. *See also* exercises and activities
rejection, 13, 86
Rendón, L. I., 200
reputation, 7, 16, 18, 25, 60, 136
resilience: burnout-resilience workshops, 28–29; colleague connections and peer support, 43–45, 144–50; combating burnout and, 121, 209–10; meaningfulness and, 91–92; pillars of, 19; purpose and, 84; self-compassion and, 110, 124–33; support groups and friendships, 150–56. *See also* balance
resistance-in-place, 51–52, 179
rest as a priority, 170–73. *See also* sleep
re-thinking thoughts and emotions, 127–28
retreat experience, 200–202
Robertson, Noelle, 13
Ross, Catherine, 193, 200
Rubin, Gretchen, 213
Rudenga, Kristi, 63–65, 67–68
rumination, 105, 126, 129, 218

Sabagh, Zaynab, 28, 48, 139
Saroyan, Alenoush, 28, 48, 139
satisficing, 130
saying no, 176–78, 197, 208–9
Schaufeli, Wilmar: on burnout, 8, 45, 73; on engagement with work, 92; on exhaustion, 114, 122; on unresolved conflict, 144
Science (magazine), 14–15
second jobs. *See* side gigs
Segal, Katherine, 87, 131
self-awareness and self-exploration, 205; activities, 210–21. *See also* reflection
self-care, 128–33, 167–73, 180, 198, 208
self-compassion, 124–33, 216
self-esteem, 64, 73, 128
selfishness to avoid burnout, 195–97
self-talk, 5–6, 70, 125–27, 129–30, 161, 220–21
self-worth, 5, 27, 58
service labor, 57
sexism. *See* gender
sexual harassment, 40–41
Sgoutas-Emch, Sanda, 197
shame: ADHD and, 118; burnout diagnosis and, 4, 25–26; emotional accessibility and, 112–13;

emotional exhaustion and, 110; external motivations and, 85; health issues and, 7; higher education as calling versus job and, 19; imposter syndrome and, 67, 120; perfectionism and, 70
Shane, Kryss, 165–67
side gigs, 3, 62, 102, 178
16 Personalities quiz, 213
sleep, 6, 9, 15, 94, 96, 171, 208
Small-Group Instructional Diagnosis, 195
Snodgrass, Jennifer, 94–97, 146, 153–54, 176
SOAR analysis, 217
social class, 76–78
social justice, 97–99
social media, 178–79
social significance, 59
social support, 150–56. *See also* connection
Sonnentag, Sabine, 181–82
Starfish Reflection, 221
Steiner, Lindsay, 36
stress, 7–9, 75, 91, 168–69, 172–73, 196
students: cheating, 123; emotional labor of supporting, 108–10, 113–14; first-generation, 76–78; help-seeking of, 121; overwork, normalization of, 175; purpose and, 92–97; social justice advocacy and, 97–99; student-faculty partnerships, 195
Success Pack exercise, 217–18
suicidal ideation, 8, 99
support groups and friendships, 42, 150–56; importance of, 144–46; peer support, 43–45
survey on burnout, 25
sustainable careers, 88–89

teaching-renewal retreats, 200–202
teambuilding, 38
tenure-track faculty versus adjunct faculty. *See* adjunct and non-tenure-track (NTT) faculty
Terosky, Aimee LaPointe, 16
therapy, 1–3, 27–28, 55, 84, 133–34; acceptance and commitment therapy (ACT), 125–26, 216
Thomason, Timothy, 164–65
Thompson, Julia, 43, 156, 171
Thompson, Michelle Dionne, 38–39, 98–99, 207–9
thriving, 45
Tomic, Welko, 90
transparency, 37, 114
trauma, 87–88, 206
tribalism, 66–67
Type A personalities, 69

unhappy achievers, 58
Universal Design for Learning (UDL), 199
unresolved conflict, 3, 14, 144

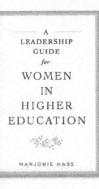

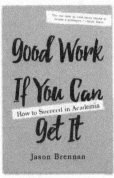